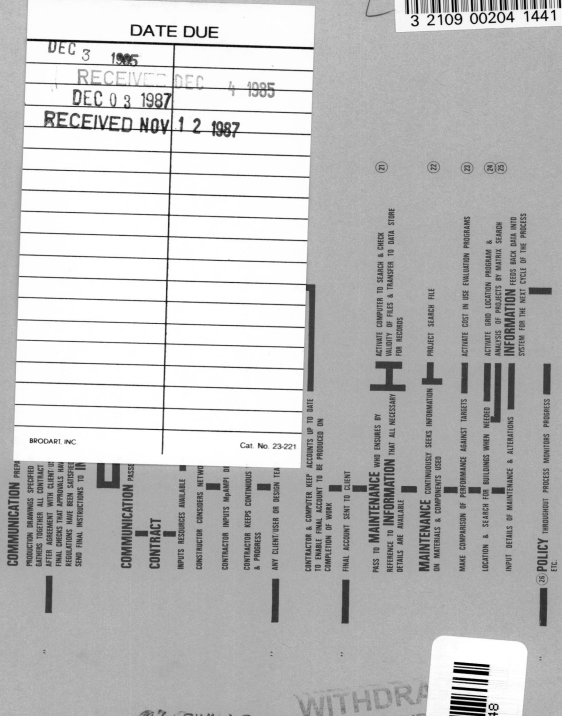

DATE DUE

DEC 3 1985	
RECEIVED DEC 4 1985	
DEC 0 3 1987	
RECEIVED NOV 1 2 1987	

BRODART, INC. Cat. No. 23-221

(15) ACTIVATE ALPHA-NUMERIC & GRAPHIC PRINTING PROCESSES.

PRINTOUTS TO CLIENT/USER. AFTER AGREEMENT SEND FOR STATUTORY APPROVALS.

FINAL EVALUATION & PROCESSING INPUT DETAILS OF STRUCTURE INPUT DETAILS OF MECHANICAL ELECTRICAL. INPUT OF FINAL SYMBOLS TO REPRESENT COMPONENTS & THEIR LOCATION & PASS TO

(16) STRUCTURAL EVALUATION PROGRAM
(17) MECH ELEC EVALUATION PROGRAM
(18) SYMBOL BLOB MpAMPIPr PROCESSING

COMMUNICATION

COMMUNICATION PREPA

PRODUCTION DRAWINGS SPECIFIED GATHERS TOGETHER ALL CONTRACT AFTER AGREEMENT WITH CLIENT/US FINAL CHECKS THAT APPROVALS HAV REGULATIONS HAVE BEEN SATISFIED SEND FINAL INSTRUCTIONS TO IN

COMMUNICATION PASSE

CONTRACT

INPUTS RESOURCES AVAILABLE

CONSTRUCTOR CONSIDERS NETWO

CONTRACTOR INPUTS MpAMPI DI

CONTRACTOR KEEPS CONTINUOUS & PROGRESS

ANY CLIENT/USER OR DESIGN TEA

CONTRACTOR & COMPUTER KEEP ACCOUNTS UP TO DATE TO ENABLE FINAL ACCOUNT TO BE PRODUCED ON COMPLETION OF WORK

FINAL ACCOUNT SENT TO CLIENT

(21) ACTIVATE COMPUTER TO SEARCH & CHECK VALIDITY OF FILES & TRANSFER TO DATA STORE FOR RECORDS

(22) PROJECT SEARCH FILE

PASS TO **MAINTENANCE** WHO ENSURES BY REFERENCE TO **INFORMATION** THAT ALL NECESSARY DETAILS ARE AVAILABLE

MAINTENANCE CONTINUOUSLY SEEKS INFORMATION ON MATERIALS & COMPONENTS USED

(23) ACTIVATE COST IN USE EVALUATION PROGRAMS

MAKE COMPARISON OF PERFORMANCE AGAINST TARGETS

(24) ACTIVATE GRID LOCATION PROGRAM &
(25) ANALYSIS OF PROJECTS BY MATRIX SEARCH

LOCATION & SEARCH FOR BUILDINGS WHEN NEEDED

INFORMATION FEEDS BACK DATA INTO SYSTEM FOR THE NEXT CYCLE OF THE PROCESS

INPUT DETAILS OF MAINTENANCE & ALTERATIONS

(26) **POLICY** THROUGHOUT PROCESS MONITORS PROGRESS ETC.

Information Methods

Information Methods

For design and construction

John Paterson
Department of Construction Management
University of Reading

Illustrations by Pamela Paterson

A Wiley – Interscience Publication

JOHN WILEY & SONS

London · New York · Sydney · Toronto

Library of Congress Cataloging in Publication Data:

Paterson, John.
    Information methods, for design and construction.

    'A Wiley–Interscience publication.'
    Bibliography: p.
    Includes index.
    1. Construction industry — Management. I. Title.

TH438.P34   658'.99   76 - 29649

ISBN 0 471 99449 9

Printed in Great Britain

CONTENTS

PREFACE

Building processes have become lengthier and more complex at a time when there is a need for simplification and speed. As it is possible that this is due not only to the vast increase in the data to be handled, but to the fact that this data is being handled by systems and processes which were developed for another age, it is proposed to examine the whole process. A process which starts with the vague idea in the mind of the proposer that a building might be necessary, to its completion, occupation, maintenance and possible demolition.

As Renaissance concepts have led to the reinforcement of the traditional view that there were absolutes which when discovered could form the basis of a perfection in all things, and that these views are often still inherent in the system of design, it is necessary to begin with a re-examination of our approach to knowledge and data. This re-examination may not only have an effect upon the systems we use, but upon the buildings and environments we create, for instead of looking for perfect systems giving perfect solutions, which must always be one person's view, we may find it more fruitful to have a flexible system to give personal expression in those areas which are most necessary. The scope of the subject matter is vast, and because of this, the subject can only be dealt with at a general level, but it is hoped that it may stimulate interest and discussions on a holistic approach to the problems of design and construction methods.

Increasing specialization, brought about by a need to try and handle the vast increase in quantity of data has tended to obscure the basic problem. This, together with the fear of losing control in a changing situation, tends to cause an entrenchment and even mechanisation of the traditional process, even when this is no longer a viable process. This in itself can bring the industry to a critical state but, when allied to educational processes, may take a long time to correct. One must feel sorry for today's students trying to find their way through a wilderness which only a few years ago was a comparatively simple process.

I believe that it is possible to develop information systems which will provide an opportunity for the user as well as the design team to make a greater contribution to the environment, and that through this a new and exciting industry can develop.

A personal abhorrence of technical terms means that the reader will not be faced with any complicated or specialist terminology.

I should like to thank Bernard Peters and other members and former members of the staff of West Sussex County Council who either provided me with an opportunity or helped me to develop some of the work described. Also Harry Atherton, Professor Biggs, Professor Bennett and Ted Cogswell for their comments on my draft, as well as T. R. Roberts, Borough Architect and Planning Officer, of the London Borough of Hackney. Finally, my greatest appreciation to my wife, who not only suffered the writing but also typed the draft and drew all of the illustrations.

June 1976

John Paterson
Privett, Hants, U.K.

INTRODUCTION

There are few who do not treasure their traditions and resent change, the introduction of new ideas, new products and new solutions. Invariably, the development of some new idea or some new process will spark off a nostalgia for the past, where, so it is often dreamed, there was no change. This nostalgia is nowhere more apparent than in the processes of architecture and construction, probably because they are so closely involved with our everyday lives, and with tradition. Such close involvement, together with the great age of the industry, has meant that methods, once functional, have now not only been traditionalized, but have been taken for granted to such a degree that we can no longer abstract ourselves enough to see the original purpose.

In addition, we cannot help choosing the appropriate set of rose-coloured spectacles when looking at any problem. In any of our activities, we crudely categorize our thoughts as follows:

Things that we hope will happen and will happen.
Things that we hope won't happen and will happen.
Things that we hope will happen and won't happen.
Things that we hope won't happen and won't happen.

Obviously the last two can be dismissed because they don't happen and don't affect our society or ourselves. But of the first two we will act creatively on the things that we want to happen, but fortify our reasoning from any possible source in order that we may persuade ourselves that the things we do not want to happen will not happen, no matter how obviously the stream of human progress may be moving in that direction.

If one imagines a horse-carriage designer in the late nineteenth and early twentieth century watching the growth of small motor car manufacturers and seeing many of them going bankrupt, he must have found it very easy to persuade himself that his beautiful craftsmanship would prevail for ever. But in fact his disappearance happened very quickly in the final result.

Are we adopting a similar attitude to the industrialization of building, new information and management techniques, computer aids and other similar developments, which have so far not been very successful? It is important that we should survey the whole scene with as little prejudice against future change as it is possible for us to have, so that we can either recognize the changes ahead, or learn by the failures that have happened.

The history of architecture is a history of slow technological change for which our ancestors fought and worked hard in a very practical way but looking back, we only see the nostalgia of the end product. In fact, many of the things which are assumed to be fundamental are comparatively recent. Professional Institutes themselves are but one example of a comparatively recent innovation supplanting a previous system with, no doubt, great forebodings and misgivings felt by those who were involved. Building itself has changed a great deal but it is more often the processes which change the most. The majority of buildings are still comparatively simple, but the problems of design and construction communications have become incredibly complex over quite a short period. Even one generation ago, large complex buildings were erected quickly and with very little documentation, but today the whole industry is increasingly burdened with the problem of handling vast quantities of data, which not only tend to become ends in themselves, but also slow down the process and increase the risks of failures, which can now be seen as an increasing problem.

In an endeavour to deal with this problem, specialists with sub-specialisms, and sub-sub-specialisms have grown up to enable one area alone to be contained within the limited scope of a single human brain, and this has only increased the complications in communication. Various methods such as interdisciplinary team working have been developed to try and find a solution, but each solution, though good in itself, has only created the next problem and almost always the result has been a lengthening of the design and construction process.

It has been argued, particularly by Architects, that the process should be a long one in order that full time and consideration can be given to a problem of such great importance in our lives. But in an age when everything is 'instant', and it is very difficult to find exceptions to this trend, can the Construction Industry stand unique as a large industry providing a bespoke service? Almost everything which might have been custom built, thirty years ago or more, from clothing to oil tankers, have become products to be bought 'off the shelf''. Is it likely that the Construction Industry will remain the only major industry to resist this social trend? Furthermore, the society which has created the 'instant' product is itself the same society for which buildings are designed, a society with a loss of faith in the future providing an atmosphere of 'live now pay later'. Mobility of labour means that an average family in the United Kingdom will have moved, according to mortgaging statistics, every seven years, whilst in the United States of America the figure is down to five years.

This creates a major problem of response time. It is probable that building construction times, on average, haven't changed dramatically since the Middle Ages; but the satisfaction of our needs has almost certainly been slowed down substantially. For example, in a small static community it is easy to see the future effect of a rise in the birth rate, and plan and build for its effect. But in a large mobile society it is possible that the arrival of a large industrial plant can suddenly create a demand for houses and schools and so on, which need instant or almost instant solutions.

If the demand becomes more instant whilst the communications get slower because of unnecessary processes, then that society and its industries will move from crisis to crisis. The effects of slow response times such as this can be seen in the butter mountains and wine lakes of the recent past.

2

This type of crisis not only has its effect on society but upon individual organizations.

The general outcome is a feeling of lack of control accompanied by a nostalgia and romanticizing of primitive methods. William Morris and his followers reacted in this way against the new industrialization of their time and today there are similar philosophies promoting alternative technologies. Whilst it is necessary to have such re-examinations to remind us of the basic way of life from which we have developed, it would be naive to think that these approaches alone can possibly solve the frightening problems which lie ahead. We will have to use more technology (not necessarily of the old type), not less, if we are going to survive. The problems caused by our limited resources of fossil fuels will certainly not be solved by primitive technologies. Similarly we shall not house the additional people yet to be born between now and the end of the century by present methods, let alone housing those people already on the planet, the majority of whom have totally inadequate or no accommodation at all. Escapism may have a small effect upon style or fashion, as the work of William Morris did, but it does little towards changing the built environment or human habitation in general. Furthermore, many of these romantic proposals are based on a return to country life at a time when even a cursory look at the world's population movements shows that we are becoming a world of urban communities at an incredible rate. There is a 4.5 per cent growth in urban areas as opposed to 2.5 per cent growth in rural areas which, against the background of a world population estimated growth from 3,000,000,000 to 7,000,000,000 by the year 2000 AD means that by that time, more people are likely to live in urban areas than rural areas. Why is this? Is it because, when given a choice carrying out primitive tasks on the land for a low income is forsaken for almost any alternative? A rise in the application for allotments is sometimes quoted as showing a trend back to the land but against the statistics quoted above, and put into their proper context, they only show that a leisure activity should not be confused with an income raising activity. Whilst the arguments for stopping any more progress goes on, governments, faced with the problem of actually housing those without any shelter at all, have been calling for procedures which will speed up the process of house building. How long will it be before the public makes similar demands for all buildings? An examination of the period between 1928 and 1932 shows that a deep recession will spark off major changes. The Construction Industry of the 1930's became quite different from that of the 1920's.

Against such backgrounds it would appear to be, at the very least, prudent to reconsider the problem we are dealing with, rather than sophisticate the solutions we have.

But to improve communications and the processing of information, it is essential to look at the whole rather than the parts, because, as so often already happens, it is easy to improve the efficiency of the parts whilst reducing the efficiency of the whole. Professions, for example, can improve the processes within their control but in so doing create greater inefficiency at the interface with other professions. The greatest interface problem is, of course, with the user with whom full participation becomes more and more necessary. The sophistication of isolated parts without reference to the objective leads again to increasing specializations, already seen to be a pro-

3

blem for other reasons, and as with natural evolutionary processes, lead finally to extinction. Not only does the basic law of nature apply to animals but also to institutions. Nowhere does it notice more than with the Guilds, which, through extreme specialization lost the great power which they held in the Middle Ages to become what they are now, very often little more than gentlemen's clubs. It is not impossible for the same thing to happen to the professions if they become inundated with the problem of increasing data reducing response times. The processes discussed are not the only ones, and not necessarily the best, but it is hoped that they will show that by strict concentration on the basic objectives and complete integration of the processes, significant improvements in time, economics and functional performance can be achieved.

It will be argued by many that the quality of work will suffer and this must obviously be carefully debated but before doing this, some factors which affect our views on quality, must be borne in mind.

1. Everyone prefers the small shop with its personal service, but it is the supermarket that gets the majority of the custom. We make our choices on a cost benefit basis, and influence change as customers.
2. Every new form of architecture was looked upon as a retrograde step, a loss of artistry or a loss of craftsmanship, but these new forms always came to be venerated by subsequent generations. Georgian and Victorian architecture each suffered vilification in their turn, but eventually became beloved by later generations. More recently, the suburbia and ribbon development of the 1930's, which caused the introduction of some of our planning laws because of public disgust, have even been praised.
3. Even the greatest adversaries of mass production enjoy its products but when these products are from an earlier period, such as sewing machines, chamber pots, toys, and even advertisements, they are often raised to the level of an art form and acquire descriptive names such as treen.
4. The massive increase in the world's population and its building needs, in addition to its present building needs, will not be solved by traditional methods.
5. If we peel away the nostalgia from our eyes, we may find new techniques as exciting as our forebears found in the Renaissance and new materials more beautiful even than the so-called traditional ones. If and when these processes and materials are clearly seen, they may engender an integrity in building which can be a heritage for future generations.

Acts of Parliament, Building Regulations and all the other chains set upon the Industry, will not go away; they can only be brought under control and for this the whole process has to be seen as a whole.

The building process began when primitive man needed protection from the climate, attack and other functional needs. As an individual, it was a simple matter for him to see around him the materials which were available for building his home and to work out a way of putting them together.

There was immediate feedback of an unsatisfactory system and a new method could be tried until the best solution for that time and with those materials was found. Again, immediate feedback told him of his success or

stone-age man

18th century man

20th century man

Figure 1

failure because the whole mechanism was going on within the mind of one individual.

It took many centuries for this simple process to change significantly for, even by the eighteenth century, the problem was still at such a scale that it could be encompassed by one man and the information flow was something which could be contained within the minds of a few people. It is only comparatively recently that we have had a situation where we have multiple client/ users, employing multiple design teams to design constructions which will be carried out by multiple contractors and sub-contractors.

This development has meant that the processes originally contained within one human mind have been stretched out, not only by a division of labour, but of mental creativity and feedback. The chain of communication can be considered in two parts. That which starts with the evaluation of the brief and ends with the completed building, and the other in the interplay of visual communication between the completed building and the designer and user.

Even if the communication system enabled the client/users to make known their views about their buildings to the design team, the response time is so slow that it could have little benefit to subsequent client users. The gradual extension and specialization of the system has created another situation which may in the end turn out to be the most significant reason for change.

When the information flow was simple, the feedback of failure was immediate, as previously explained. Even when the system became more complex, as in the eighteenth and nineteenth centuries, it could still work with reasonable safety providing that the system of building only changed slowly. Apprentices, pupils and others grew up within the profession or trade, learning by day-to-day experience about their work, so that they took over responsibility with a substantial background of practical training and experience.

In this century, two things have happened at the same time which are critical for building design and construction. Firstly, there has been a wave of new materials being used in an infinite variety of ways and in this extended situation it means that the whole team can be learning and practising on almost every building. Added to this, is a change in the education processes of the team. For other and very good reasons, members of the team are now trained in schools, colleges and Universities and because of the speed with which new materials and techniques are developed, they can only be taught the principles of building rather than a vocational craft or trade. Even the principles must be fairly general if the student is not to be trained in a technology which will be out of date before he is qualified. In this situation, members throughout the building team can become qualified, and reach senior positions of responsibility with very little practical knowledge of building with its possible success or failure. Before this new system of education and rapid change in methods of building, an Architect, Quantity Surveyor, Engineer, Contractor or anyone else in the chain would feel competent to challenge what he might think to be a mistake. In the new situation of rapidly changing techniques, not only will each member of the team feel unqualified to comment on another member's contribution, but probably would not recognize a mistake anyway. The Contractor adopts a position of doing what he is told, and expects more and more documentation in order to cover himself. The Clerk of Works is forced more and more into becoming an onlooker, because even if he had the knowledge of a Building Research Establishment, he would be quite unable to judge and test every new situation with which he is faced. This must inevitably mean an increase in the rate of building failure if the present systems continue.

If we can speed up the process, at least the views of client/users and the rest of the team can be fed back into the system that much more quickly so that it might have an effect on an earlier succeeding generation of buildings than otherwise would have happened.

But in order to speed the process, the process itself must be understood, and to do this, some aspects of human thought will have to be considered as it is within the human brain that the whole problem lies for both the creator and the user.

Just as the anatomical research of artist/scientists such as Leonardo da Vinci and Michelangelo during the Renaissance eventually found its outlet in the supplementation of the muscle power of the human body in the Industrial Revolution; so also is the research of the last hundred years or so, into the workings of the human mind, beginning to have its effect on supplementing, and reinforcing the human brain. This is having the same disruptive effects on society as the Industrial Revolution had, but there is no avoiding the issue. If it were possible to stop the world population increase and stop the rest of the world wanting a better standard of living, the western world could perhaps look for more romantic ways of solving our problems, but in the circumstances we must accept the challenge and face the problem.

Unfortunately any suggestion of supplementing our mental resources meets the fear that machines will supplant the human brain. These fears have probably been enhanced by the early successes with computers which encouraged some researchers and journalists to overreach themselves in both their ambitions and their phraseology. Terms such as electronic brains helped to create a feeling that computers would soon take over. Unfortunately there is still a residue of this approach in the large amount of work that has been put into computer research directed towards the creative aspects of building, and the relatively small amount into information processing of everyday activities.

This is a great pity, not only because the creative parts are the most enjoyable parts to do, but because the human brain will do them best for a long time to come.

It is in information retrieval and processing where the greatest need for research lies, and where we could be freed from the drudgeries of search and boredom of repetitiveness, and hopefully it would enable us to apply a new creativeness over the whole spectrum of the industry.

Throughout, the emphasis will be upon the belief that because of the slowness of evolution, as far as man is concerned, it can be assumed that his fundamental needs do not change: only the means by which he satisfies those needs change. Reference to any ancient writings will show how little humanity has changed for several thousand years, and therefore, if we can get some idea of how our thinking processes operate, it might be possible to create systems which are more compatible with our normal way of working and which are likely to serve our needs for a longer time.

On the basis of an examination of man's needs and his thinking processes, an examination of the information flow will be made and possible alternatives offered. This examination may be rather painful because, due to the upsurge of specialisms already referred to, confusion has been added to confusion by many members of the team developing their own languages. This situation was brought out in the two Tavistock Institute reports in 1965 and 1966 'Communications in the Building Industry' and 'Interdependence and Uncertainty', which can only leave the reader wondering how any building could be achieved at all. Design, in the sense of aesthetic judgements, is not the subject of this book, but it is impossible to divorce the process from the product. Furthermore, design, in the sense of it being an act of creation, is very much a part of this thesis because design, in its broadest sense, is an activity which is applied to, say, the creation of a management or information structure, as much as to the design of a building.

In any case, so far as design in architecture is concerned, it is possible that we have confused our examination of the problem of building by grouping together all types of building and calling them Architecture, which has then caused confusion in the information flow. It is suggested that in this context it would be equally unrealistic to assume that custom-built car firms, mass production car firms, and garages, were all the same and should have the same treatment and processes, and for that matter, education and training.

It can be seen that Architecture falls into three main and very dissimilar categories (Figure 2).

In the first category is the prestigious building, which in the past was the only type of building referred to as Architecture. These are the special buildings which must be of the highest creative quality and serve to inspire society even at the expense of functional efficiency.

Then there is the second category, which constitutes the major part of our

a. Prestige

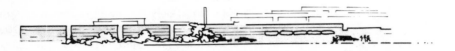

b. General

c. Infill

Figure 2

building expenditure and which includes housing, hospitals, schools and similar buildings where functional performance and efficiency, and the speedy satisfaction of user needs are paramount. It is to this category that this book is mainly, but not exclusively, directed.

Lastly there are the infill buildings, conservation in our existing towns and villages, and so on, and this section increasingly revolves around a craft/servicing industry.

In addition to this complication of description, the process of design has become inextricably bound up with the process of communicating the design, which itself has become confused by mixing together the communication of the design with its pricing.

There are two main aspects of the design information for construction. Firstly there is the communication of the designer's intention to those who will convert the synthesized design concepts into an artefact for use by others. The second is the communication of such of the designer's intentions to the Contractor as to enable a price to be agreed between the client and the Contractor. These levels of communication are assumed to be the same, but it is intended to show that they can be quite different.

Before design can commence, there must also be a flow of information and so therefore what is needed is a completely integrated and logically organized data system, which will provide for each participant a flow of rapidly produced and understandable communications. It would be attractive to supplant one set of idealistic rules which don't work, for another set. To put the world right is everyone's dream. To avoid this, a data bank is proposed which would grow naturally from basic human functions and their criteria, rather than the creation of one person's ideal.

The design should proceed by a series of logical steps, each member concentrating on providing and receiving information at each particular stage of the work, in the required order and without gaps. Also, the information flow should be controlled through all its stages by progressively reducing the criteria, again step by step, thereby limiting the areas of enquiry to those which will meet the specific requirements and excluding those which will not. The aim is to examine in some detail the essential characteristics of such a system, and to construct a framework for a process which will provide for each participant that which he needs for his own area of work.

At the outset, in defining and refining a rational and applicable system, it is necessary to look for those common factors which run through the design/construct process. This leads to the realization that all work is based on human activities: activities of the occupiers or users which build up the brief, those of the designers and of the constructors and makers of the parts of the physical structure, and its surroundings. Recognition of this factor has far-reaching consequences in defining a rational breakdown of major operations into manageable steps, and this leads to the following recurring factors:

MANPOWER
ACTIVITY
MATERIAL
PLANT

These properties set up a standard framework for classification of any activity and encompasses all that is needed to be known about it. Thus it can be used on a comparative basis as a design tool, cost planning, network scheduling and assessment in production, and planning and controlling work content in construction. Even after the completion of the building it may be used for the feedback of actual time and costs to benefit future operations.

Construction management should emanate logically by using these factors for the communication of the design teams intentions. The ability for this to happen will be examined.

Maintenance management, a grossly overlooked subject, must be seen as part of the cycle and not as an appendage. Conservation of existing building stock, and the proper use of resources in future building stock, make it essential that maintenance management must be raised to the same level of management as the other parts of the process. In fact, it may be necessary in the future to consider maintenance servicing as part of the initial contract to build. After all, this happens in a lot of other industries. A shortage of labour for the maintenance of buildings may force rapid changes in this area.

Sometimes it is suggested that economic recession will bring a flood of cheap labour back into the maintenance of the buildings, but this is as unrealistic as expecting a return to any other similar tasks which attract a social stigma of menial work. There are a large number of employments which, in spite of the inducements of high pay, do not attract applicants because they have now become socially unacceptable. It is the examination of this sort of problem for which a category called POLICY (Chapter 8) is created.

One of the unfortunate side effects of a surfeit of information is that efficiency can actually fall at the same time as knowledge increases. This is due to the inability to even handle the information, let alone use it, and this in turn means that it is so simple to gradually slip back in the moving tide of information flow. There is an expression 'Why is there always time to put things right, when there is no time to do the job properly in the first place?'. This becomes increasingly true as senior management spends more and more of its time dealing with the mistakes of yesterday, and never finding time to look at tomorrow's problems, so that these in turn become a further noose around the neck of management. This way leads to ever worsening problems as each successive wave of decisions becomes more and more unrealistic and frenetic.

The energy crisis was a typical example of this approach. Whilst architects were designing buildings with vast areas of glass, very often in opposition to the desires of society, the facts of the situation about fossil fuels were readily available but either ignored, or not known to them. In the flurry of day to day management, the outdated fashions of an earlier period were being re-peated without re-examination. The same thing is still happening in other areas, and it is not until a subject reaches crisis proportions that time will be found to consider them. This will happen with maintenance, water re-sources, site labour and so on. That is not to say that fashion, as the glass era was, is not important, because it seems that as it is impossible for our brains to find a simple direction within the infinite amount of data at our disposal, we use fashion as a sort of mental coat hanger upon which we can hang other information. This will be dealt with again later.

It is difficult to separate style and fashion, as it appears to depend more upon the subject to which it applies, rather than anything else, but the fact remains that Architecture has been a succession of styles. From a designer's point of view, a style must be rather like pelmanism. For example, it is easier to remember facts if they are associated with places. There are many systems of a similar nature and it would seem likely that architects cannot, no matter how much they think otherwise, start with an open mind on any design, purely from the fact that the whole world of data is too large an area from which to choose, and also because they cannot remember data un-less it is related to a style.

Whilst it may be impossible to anticipate the next style, it is possible to study trends, and it is this, amongst other things, which POLICY should do. For example when designing buildings on a sixty year loan period with large areas of glass is it not reasonable to find time to consider whether the educational system will produce window cleaners over the same period? This is only an isolated example of the problems which will be studied in a little more depth; there are others, such as the future of site labour, technicians and so on. An office or organization must find its own direction and not sit back and wait to be buffeted by events as they occur. It cannot be left to an Institute or similar organization, because by their very nature, they can only react to a situation, not create a new environment in which things can happen.

A policy group, given the opportunity to examine itself, could quickly see that if one put together the data required for quite an average job, to ensure that all reasonable facets had been examined, the scale of data would be quite enormous and utterly beyond the possible absorption and checking by the design team. Because it is impossible to handle these large quantities of data, speculations are made with rough checks to ensure that the major points have been covered, but only too often, as has been seen, this leaves the team vulnerable to increasing legal action and client dissatisfaction. As society is demanding higher levels of knowledge of every aspect of our work, while at the same time the amount of available knowledge is increasing, it is inevitable that the amount of real and claimed failure of the participants in the industry will increase at a vast rate purely because of the inability of the human brain to handle, in a practical way, the required quantities of information. For example, an architect who was until fairly recently considered to be more of an artist in the eyes of the law, is now increasingly seen to be a specialist in the design and construction of buildings. This in turn assumes that he should know all the regulations, codes of practice and latest scientific research not only in design, but in construction and materials as well.

Something must obviously be done to help the team, as the production of more and more regulations and data will not be stopped. Human beings are, amongst other things, data handling machines, each one of varying efficiency. Whilst they are likely to be the only means we have for heuristic sensing of mass information for a long time to come, they are far less efficient in such aspects as large scale memory storage and repetitive calculation, and it is to these areas that we must look for help from machines and new techniques.

It has been unfortunate that management, in its desperate efforts to stay afloat in the rising tide of paper, has either neglected these possibilities or put them in the hands of someone who has little or no experience of the basic jobs to be carried out, and even if able to find them out, has no power of implementation. Add to this the fact that very often the decision to use a computer has been followed up by using inexperienced programmers rather than using professional expertise. This has created two situations which may become serious for the industry.

Firstly, the inexperienced can only examine what they see to be happening and not what should be happening. Secondly, by using amateurs in computing, the level of achievement has been far below that possible, with inevitable economic consequences.

With an industry so complex and so comprehensive as the Construction Industry in most parts of the world, it is extremely difficult to see what should be happening, and there is little doubt that only management is in a position even to try. If they can spend some of their time in this area of study, it may enable them to free themselves more and more from day to day crises and to give time to plan ahead. In those cases where computers are needed, liaison with system analysts and programmers can easily be organized to provide the link with management intentions. The implications of this and the effect of setting up such computer systems will be discussed, together with possible advantages and disadvantages. The last chapter will deal with the possible implications for the future.

There is now an opportunity, never before possible, to create a flexible and dynamic environment which could be very different from the imposed ideal of a few individuals, and making this period the end, perhaps, of the Renaissance idea of Man at the Centre of the Universe. Gosling, writing on the music of John Cage, says:

'One day in 1917 a French artist called Marcel Duchamp took a porcelain urinal, signed it "R. Mutt" and submitted it to an exhibition in New York. 35 years later, in the same city, John Cage presented a composition called "4'33"", in which for four and a half minutes a pianist sat at his instrument in perfect silence. Today Duchamp is rated as important to twentieth-century art as Picasso . . . Is it fair to compare these two apostles of the absurd? . . . Both the examples I have mentioned were the tips of a long and deadly intellectual process. They resulted from a rare gift of pushing an idea way beyond the normal limits of acceptability. The impulse to do so arose from a dissatisfaction with the whole concept of Fine Art, seeing it as an artificial edifice, mirroring a society based on a monarchical system, with a ruler at the centre of a structure containing components of gradually descending importance (the favourite triangle of the Renaissance painters recalls the musical scale with its 'dominant' note).

Duchamp deliberately undermined this idea by using a humble, machine made artefact quite purposelessly. And in the same way Cage tried to remove the class distinctions between music and noise by making his silent "4'33"" a mere frame into which outside noises could enter as full collaborators — another example of artistic democracy.

In a further expression of revulsion against the Renaissance idea of Man at the centre of the universe, with the Artist as his special champion, Cage tries desperately to keep himself out of his work. He sees humanity in a way which corresponds more closely to modern scientific views — and also to Oriental philosophy — as a modest part of the total flux, and regards himself rather as a door-opener than as a dictatorial moulder and shaper.'

The same might be said of Architecture in the future, if we could release ourselves from Renaissance traditions of hierarchical thought structures, design egoism, and absolutism in our methodologies, and allow greater freedom for personal expression in the environment.

Chapter 1
MAN: DESIGNER AND USER

Even though our thinking processes are not at present capable of simulation, it is necessary for some examination to be made of both the way we appear to think and our concepts of knowledge and data. To do this, it is necessary to try and bring together some ideas about ourselves and our world, and to create a hypothesis which will constitute a point of departure: these ideas are described as thoughts because, as the proposition is made in this chapter, any idea can only be considered as a temporary working hypothesis. And so these thoughts will constitute the 'rules' upon which the propositions made in this book are based.

Thought 1
Knowledge is infinite. Even today it is not uncommon for it to be believed that if research is pursued relentlessly enough in any given direction, one will eventually come to an absolute truth or kernel. It was not very long ago that scientists believed that at one end of the spectrum of knowledge was the atom, and at the other was what turned out to be our galaxy, but as time has shown, every new 'kernel' can again be opened to produce yet another kernel. And so we must visualise knowledge not as a set of facts, but more like an infinity of Russian dolls extending in all directions.

But scientists having rectified their earlier view, still have difficulties in establishing any basic laws. Feyerabend (1975) says,

> "A scientist who wishes to maximize the empirical content of the views he holds and who wants to understand them as clearly as he possibly can, must therefore introduce other views; that is, he must adopt a pluralistic methodology. He must compare ideas with other ideas rather than with experience, and he must try to improve rather than discard the views that have failed in the competition. Proceeding in this way he will retain the theories of man and cosmos that are found in Genesis, or in the Pimander, and he will elaborate them and use them to measure the success of evolution and other "modern" views. He may then discover that the theory of evolution is not as good as is generally assumed and that it must be supplemented, or entirely replaced, by an improved version of Genesis. Knowledge so

13

conceived is not a series of self-consistent theories that converges towards an ideal view, and it is not a gradual approach to the truth: It is rather an ever-increasing *ocean of mutually incompatible (and perhaps even incommensurable) alternatives,* each single theory, each fairy tale, each myth that is part of the collection, forcing the others into greater articulation and all of them contributing, via this process of competition, to the development of our consciousness. Nothing is ever settled. No view can ever be omitted from a comprehensive account Plutarch, or Diogenes, Laertius and not Dirac, or von Neumann, are the models for presenting knowledge of this kind in which the *history* of a science becomes an inseparable part of the science itself — it is essential for its further *development* as well as for giving *content* to the theories it contains at any particular moment. Experts and laymen, professionals and dilettanti, truth freaks and liars — they are all invited to participate in the contest and to make their contribution to the enrichment of our culture. The task of the scientist, however, is no longer "to search for the truth" or "to praise god" or "to systematize observations" or "to improve predictions". These are but side effects of an activity to which his attention is now mainly directed and which is *"to make the weaker case the stronger"* as the sophists said, *and thereby to sustain the motion of the whole'.*

This is not all. Not only are we building one theory upon another, but the scientific laws which lie at the heart of the whole panorama of knowledge are themselves thrown into doubt. Feyerabend (1975) continues:

'It is well known (and has also been shown in detail by Duhem) that Newton's theory is inconsistent with Galileo's law of free fall and with Kepler's laws: that statistical thermodynamics is inconsistent with the second law of the phenomenological theory: that wave optics is inconsistent with geometrical optics; and so on.'

Feyerabend therefore suggests that basic 'truths' which form the foundations for almost all of our theories are not 'truths' at all. If we cannot find a truth or a basic law or an absolute in science how can we be certain of anything. Can there be a good architecture except to one person? Can there be preciseness on even a single fact? The acceptance of Hasenberg's Uncertainty Principle finally destroyed belief in absolutes and left every law in the position of a transient hypothesis.

Thought 2
Data depends upon its environment. Every piece of information we take hold of will vary according to the environment in which it is placed. To take an example — a simple piece of data — Ego. A person can be himself, a father, grandfather, son, uncle, etc., etc., depending not only upon the relationship to other egos, but upon which observer is considering the data, as in the diagram (Figure 3).

But even these simple multi-variable relationships can be complicated to infinity by even further variables, say murderer — victim, employer — employee, etc., etc., none of which are necessarily exclusive. Therefore the telling of a

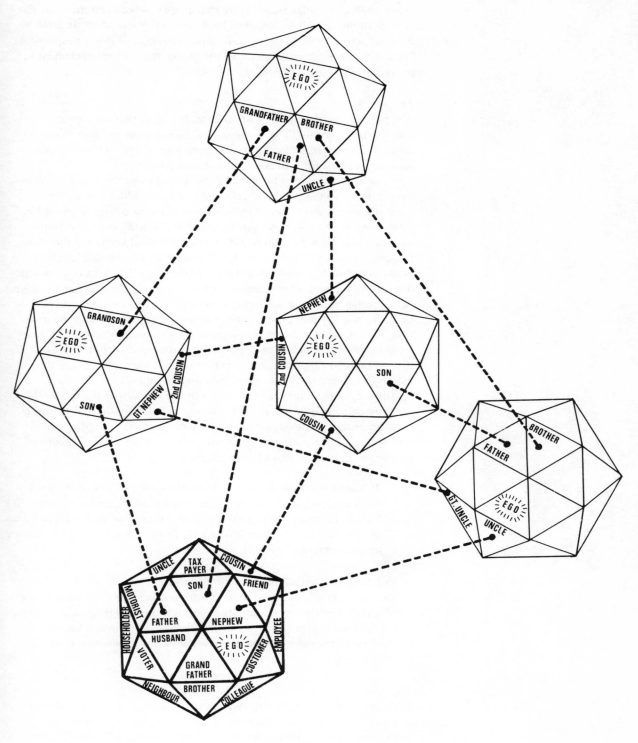

Figure 3

sworn truth can change endlessly by changing each word and therefore concept, until the truth is no longer to be defined (This is a favourite game of film and play authors: a victim seen through the eyes of many people who knew him or her, all swearing to tell the truth). It is also very pertinent to the problem of data co-ordination as we shall see later.

Thought 3
A hypothesis for the world of knowledge. It is clear that we cannot leave ourselves without any framework or foundations and that to put forward another 'truth' would be no improvement, and so the most reasonable way forward is to create a working hypothesis.

It might therefore not be unreasonable to represent the world as follows. An enormous volume of multi-coloured beans into which a new born mind is theoretically placed. This new mind has some pre-programmed information, but no previous input from the 'real world'. But it has to try and make some sense of this world of multi-coloured beans and therefore decides to explore to see if there is a 'rationale' in say the visible yellow beans, and therefore develops a theory. (After all, a theory can be worked out for any random set of numbers or information if one tries hard enough.) Now another new mind is injected into the beans but sees these yellow beans from a different position, and so the original theory has to be modified. To test the new theory, the yellow beans are excavated to see if there is a deep truth of yellow beans, but unfortunately, not only is there no pattern of yellow beans beneath the first set, but the other sides of the yellow beans turn out to be multi-coloured (Figure 4).

The only conclusion the two minds can come to is that the real world can only be what they want it to be, based on the limitations of their pre-programming, e.g. a need to rationalize randomness. (Very noticeable in architecture and planning.) There is an excitement when a new theory of patterns is discovered which Gregory calls an Aha!

> 'It is little more, perhaps never more than a reshuffling of the pack of one's concepts, to draw a new combination which shows promise. Perhaps the *aha* experience is a gasp of recognition, that the novel draw of concept cards fits surprisingly with features from the past to improv some aspects of the future.'

Koestler puts similar ideas in a different way.

Just as we have learned to live with infinite space, we must learn to live with infinite knowledge and infinite time. (It is possible that we have grown into a life form pre-programmed with a cyclical time concept because of our night/day environment, and therefore seek out time elements in the random scene.)

Thought 4
If the quantity of data is beyond rationality and we are only grabbing at a working hypothesis (Thought 1), and even this hypothesis can be destroyed by exposing a new facet of the hard data (Thought 2), how can we proceed at all? Perhaps it is advisable to look at the pre-programmed part of the mind in the hypothesis.

16

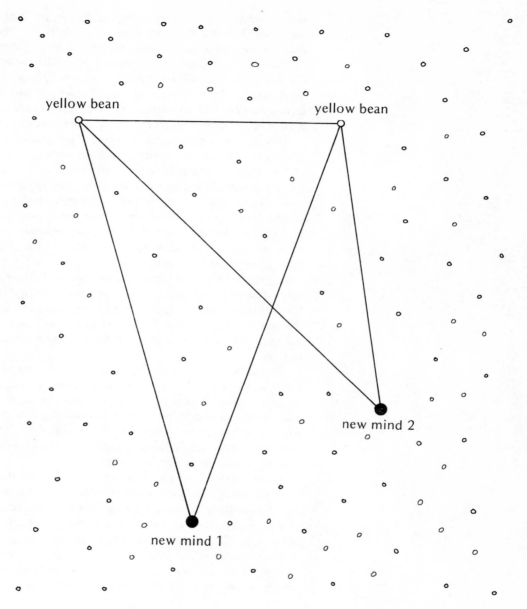

Figure 4

Because we have evolved in this particular environment, i.e. one particular area in the beans, we have proceeded from one hypothesis to the next, building up automative parts as we went along. An ant for example, would see a different set of beans and therefore would react differently to its world, causing a different evolution. Once embarked on the road of procreation and survival, the development of the mechanism is fairly obvious and has been well described elsewhere. Some examples will be useful nevertheless. If a pair of mechanisms with progeny, only have a 'program' 'eat to survive', but not one to move, then they must die when they exhaust the food with-

17

in their reach. If both 'parents' have to move to get food, then the progeny are at risk. The best 'program' therefore would be for 'mother' to stay with the progeny, whilst 'father' hunts for food. If he only develops a 'move program' without a 'get home program', he will be lost and the family will die. Therefore one early basic program must be 'pattern recognition', or in other words to feed information about his journey into a map, and have a memory upon which to imprint that map. It is also necessary to have a pattern recognition program in order that the family can be recognized.

This exposes one fundamental aspect of our problem. Because the recognition of correct sensory symbols has been a matter of survival for so much of our history, a large part of our mental effort is devoted to trying to rationalize the symbols and patterns we receive. This must lead to a need for a mechanism within us for setting up hypotheses which can be tested or discarded. It can also lead to the very human desire to create idealistic worlds; an Eldorado. Architecture and Planning can easily be seen to this type of idealization of the world. A look at the urban layout of say Chandigargh, or Milton Keynes, or the plans of Van der Rohe show the desire to create a situation in which other human beings must conform in an 'ideal' world — very different from pragmatically developed 'primitive' urban situations. Rationalizing data and forming maps and patterns in our minds is obviously the nearest thing to reality for us, and so it would seem wise to ensure that our hypothesis stays as close as possible to these types of basic activities in man.

We must of course be careful to remember that this too is only a hypothesis, and that our standards for human values are not absolute for all people, but capable of adaptation to every human being. We are all aware of many examples of primitive peoples (so-called) and some religious sects, who are able to survive in situations far outside the 'normal' range of survival and comfort levels normally used. (This becomes important when considering criteria for human activities.)

These situations, which involved going far beyond the normally accepted levels of physical endurance used to be dismissed as tricks or black magic, but are increasingly being subjected to serious consideration, so much so that they have now promoted large research programmes, particularly in Russia and America. The power that can be unleashed by changing the rules, which is the best way to describe these acts, can be seen in such instances as the 'beating of the four-minute mile'. Once a mental barrier of accepting certain rules is broken, new opportunities present themselves.

Thought 5

If we can select from so many alternatives, can there be such things as canons of architecture, or of anything else, or are these just working hypotheses? If so, how are they selected, because in this lies the object of our information systems. Is it like the selection of beans in Thought 1?

Before deciding, we should look at our existing rules. For example, is there a difference between building and architecture? If there is, what rationale constitutes architecture? Is it the difference between building being functional, and architecture being non-functional building — but architects have strived for functionalism for a long time. Should architecture be regular? If the answer is 'yes' — what of Gaudi; if the answer is 'no' — what of

18

Van der Rohe? Is it a high standard of craftsmanship? Then what of some of Le Corbusier's buildings or alternatively, what worth would Van der Rohe's buildings have with poor workmanship? Is architecture instantly recognized and enjoyed by the 'masses'? Any history of art or architecture shows that most works acclaimed by the artists are disliked by the majority. From this, one could reasonably conclude that architecture is anti-social; but quite the contrary, it is claimed to be a reflection of the society that produces it. Even from these superficial comments it is clear that architectural preferences may just as easily be one of fashion as of anything else, and furthermore, one of personal choice. After all, there are very noticeable signs that snobbishness and uniqueness are a factor, and this in turn is similar to Gregory's Aha theory. As he says:

> 'For a full strength aha, it must be (or at least seem to be) one's own novelty . . . .'

That is not to say that it is *only* fashion, but it is very probable that because the scope of possible data which could be used for selection in a design is so enormous, a fashion is needed to concentrate the mind on to a selected area upon which variations can be played until boredom moves us on to the next area. This has, after all, always been the case. Roman cities, wherever they were built, were standardized to a degree undreamed of in this so-called industrialized and standardized age. They maintained a standard design quite irrespective of climate and functional need. Why was it done? Because we as human beings are severely limited in the quantity of data we can handle. Without some outside help, *we must either standardize our ideas as the Romans did, or standardize our components and systems as we do today.*

Thought 6
Each human brain is a data storage and collecting/handling unit. Because each mind from birth, in this hypothesis, must start collecting data in a different relative position to the beans, it must inevitably become 'individual', because its data store becomes increasingly unique. Apart from this, the pre-programmed parts (heredity) may also tend to bias the area of search. This can become important in considering user-response, etc. later. Again, one is trembling on the edge of philosophical discussion of nature versus nurture, but nevertheless these areas must be considered if we are to move towards greater user participation, with all that that infers in terms of communication.

Thought 7
Some of the pre-programmed parts of our mind have an effect on our reaction to other people and other things.
Just as we would not be able to find our way back to our families without a facility for storing maps and patterns; we would have stayed in our earliest primitive state without a programmed need for pioneering and change. But equally, constant change, without a program for conserving the best of what we had learnt would have been equally disastrous. Therefore it would not be unreasonable to include in the pre-programmed part

of our hypothesis both a need for conservatism, coupled with a need for the stimulation of new ideas. This can best be seen perhaps in the relationship between a man and a woman. If one's partner never changed their expression and repeated the same sentences, one would soon become bored. But on the other hand, if one's partner constantly changed their facial expression and produced sentences made up from random words, one would certainly become very irritated because it would be impossible to bring the barrage of information under control. Here we can see the relationship to architecture and the increasing interest in semiotics in architecture, which may increase our understanding of the built environment.

From the foregoing thoughts, a further hypothesis will be proposed upon which the succeeding management tools will be based.

(a) The brain receives a selective but continuous flow of data for storage, some of whicn has to be used again frequently, some occasionally, and some never again.

(b) Where groups of data are likely to be re-used frequently (blinking an eye), the data is grouped together into a package, which we shall call a blob, ready for re-use as a complete entity rather than constantly remaking every detail of the package. It also helps to reduce storage space within the brain, as information is always held at the highest level.

(c) Where data is to be used infrequently, it is stored in multifaceted mini-blobs which are related one with another in a structure roughly as described in Thought 2.

(d) Where data is not used again, a mechanism similar to a 'times used' program used in computers is assumed. In this system a regular check is made by searching the stored files to check on how often, if ever, the data has been used. Where not used, the data is allowed to die.

(e) A blob is now assumed to be the largest unit of repetitive reusable data available.

(f) These blobs can be reused in a variety of different ways to create the newness we need, whilst retaining the core of conserved knowledge.

Example 1. Words are a blob of data. Put together repetitively gives banality. Put together in a unique way can produce sublimity or poetry, *provided* that the basic rules of preprogramming are observed.

Example 2. Pieces of building are symbols resembling words which we put together. If put together repetitively it is monotonous. If put together in a wild random form it could become irritating and tiresome. Beyond that, it would become unintelligible.

(g) Care must be taken that these blobs of information are re-examined occasionally otherwise they, and us, become outdated by the changing environment created by the other minds around us. Views parcelled up in childhood are often carried through life without being re-examined even though the situation in which they were created may have changed completely (superstitions are a case in point).

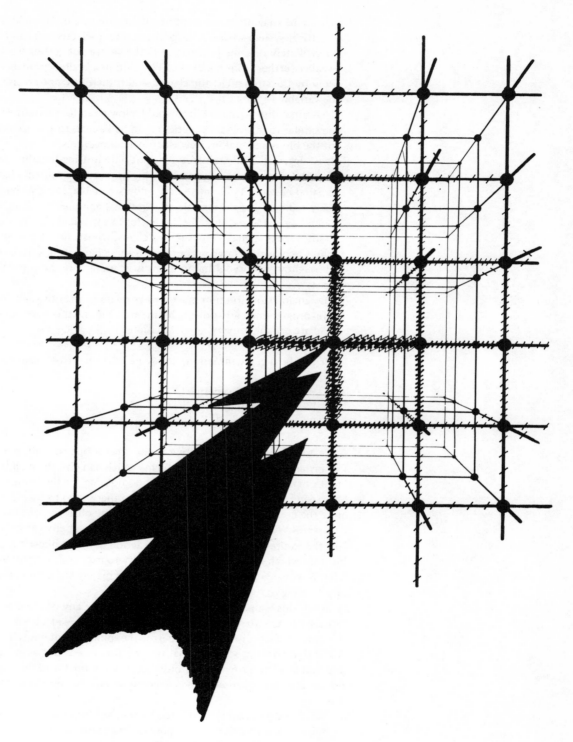

Figure 5

(h) We could imagine the concept of a data structure in Thought 2 as an electrical system where a charge is put into a selected area and a blob is immediately reformed — strongly at the centre but getting weaker and weaker further from the centre. The blob in a brain is probably defined only by the strength of the charge, and is therefore not precise and can be variable (Figure 5).

An inability to make blobs would allow a random output which would be similar to madness. Synectics could be likened to a re-examination of the blobs and making new electrical connections.

(i) It is suggested that Architecture is not only putting together basic data and blob data, but doing so in varying proportions so that a balance is created between the immediately understandable, recognizable, and possibly tedious, and the completely irrational and unrecognizable, which would be chaos and therefore resentful to the human brain which constantly seeks to make order out of chaos. Whilst the proportion of reused blobs may vary, a large proportion of these have always been reused throughout history, either in terms of manufacture, or in terms of an idea.

(j) Design and Construction must always relate to the human being and the pre-programmed areas of the brain, even though these are not absolute and are capable of very great variations.

After this further examination, it may be relevant to ask again:

What is a creative design?
What is designing?
What is a designer?

A creative design may be exciting to the creator but not to the recipient. For instance, students are set problems which can give them all the excitement of creation and exploration, but do nothing for their tutor who may have seen all the solutions before. For him there is no excitement. If we separate the creator in the act of creating from the observer, one can see that a dangerous situation can occur in Architecture whereby the creator is getting the excitement of a personal interaction between himself and his design. but that which he creates can be a penalty to user and constructor. And what is worse, with a low response time, he may never even know about any possible havoc that he may have caused.

When this happens in painting or literature, or any of the other arts, it is not a serious matter, because one does not *have* to read a book or look at a painting. In fact it is the artist's personal exploration of himself and his world that contains so much that is important in art. But with Architecture and building it is different not only because the final work has to be used, but because it is imposed upon observers and users whether they like it or not.

This basic problem is aggravated by the fact that the building design can be more or less functional, and more or less irrational, according to choice. So what is the choice? Does the user or the client who pays have a choice? Does the ordinary passer-by have a choice? Planning Committees and user participation committees try to regularize this impossible situation, but

22

can the product of such a process be considered an art form?

So what is designing? This must be the assemblage of components of varying scale. As an illustration, we may take books which have been accepted as works of art and which include those written with standard recognized words and also those of Joyce, for example, which were written using many words which he created himself. At the other end of the scale, many books are written largely with substantial extracts from other books, and so it is with architecture.

If every building component were to be redesigned all of the time, it would be as confusing as a book with every word a newly made word, which must be one of the reasons why there has been such standardization of symbols in the past: Greek, Roman, Georgian, etc. The other reason, of course, being an inability to train an industry to cope with an infinite set of variables.

Could this be the problem of today, where we too are unable to train an industry to cope with such change, and where the user and the man in the street cannot cope with such an expanding vocabulary of symbols? Never has there been such a variety, brought about by the greatest ever number of buildings being individually designed. It is generally acknowledged that small traditional villages and towns have a great charm, and that they also appear to have a great deal of variety, and from this, it might be deduced that variety equals charm.

Large cities on the other hand usually have major streets and boulevards of distinctive and repetitive buildings, and it is only within these major recognizable patterns that variety takes place. This may be tradition's unerring recognition that our pattern making programmes would find it difficult to remember the complicated patterns of small town variety on such a large scale, whilst being able to do so at small scale. For both these, and other reasons a high degree of standardization has been used throughout history.

What is a designer? If we use the definition of designing given above, then everyone is a designer. This idea would have been totally unacceptable in the nineteenth century, where creativity was a gift you were either born with or not. Whilst there is still a considerable hangover of this idea, it is increasingly accepted that everyone has creativity; but with special aptitudes in various directions. Even training is suspect, as so many of the celebrated creators avoided formal training and yet transcended the levels of those with formal training. Clearly, there are different levels by which we assess a designer. A housewife creating a meal, a householder creating his garden layout, or a child making a sand castle are certainly exercising exactly the same mechanisms as an Architect designing a building, or a Contractor creating a management organization. If everyone has a creative talent, the question which must logically arise is how far should each individual be able to design his own environment? As the works of anthropologists such as Morris (1967) have shown, the imprinting of ourselves upon our own piece of territory is still strong within us; urinating on the walls being replaced by the hanging of pictures, to let everyone know that we have established our rights over the territory. The personalization of a space in the Bürolandschaft office to identify the user of the space is often clearly noticeable.

What is the ideal of this designer or user? Is it possible that the worst thing for mankind would be for it to achieve its ideal, even if it were possible to do so, when it is the contest which is important to its survival.

Stability and uncertainty are required together in every aspect of our lives. A large part of our lives must be stable in order to allow us a feeling of security and also to allow time for exploring the uncertain areas. This balance might be obtained within a person's job, or if the job is totally stable, then insecurity is often sought in recreation, and this is again reflected in the built environment.

These aspects of design and construction have to be considered before one can consider the type and use of data. For example, there are clearly different needs for processes and data depending upon whether society will demand more or less variety in the environment. Therefore it is necessary to summarize the points discussed so far in order that a working hypothesis can be developed:

1) Out of an infinite amount of data which surrounds us, we select certain facets of information. These facets are selected because we are the mechanisms that we are, and restricted by what we are, because we have been designed and redesigned through the passage of time to select only certain pieces of data. For example, as a short sighted person, without glasses I can only see a world dimly beyond about 10 feet. Certainly there are no stars in the sky for me. But with glasses, a whole new world opens up as I see stars within our galaxy. With a telescope a new world opens up yet again as I see beyond our galaxy. But when I receive information from a radio telescope, something else happens altogether. The next logical step is to question what lies outside our senses? *Therefore the world as we know it is partly what we choose to select and partly what we have facilities for selecting.*

2) Because of the way we have developed, some choices are more compatible with ourselves than others. Sleeping on a bed of nails is possible, but not particularly compatible with the design development of the human body.

3) As human brains are choosing and handling the data, it is most likely that mechanisms which operate in similar ways to ourselves will be the most compatible.

4) We should not overburden our capacity for accepting patterns and symbols.

5) The more routine and repetitive activities can be 'parcelled up' or mechanized, giving a greater opportunity for exploring the frontiers of knowledge.

6) Because there are no absolutes, *there will be no optimum solutions for all time.* The best that can be provided is the most satisfactory hypothesis, for a particular situation, at any particular time.

7) There is an 'aha' experience for both the creator and the observer, and because of this there is the risk (though not inevitable) that the creator in architecture can enjoy his creative experience in designing a building to the detriment of the user.

8) We live by creating hypotheses of the world and making idealizations of this world, which gives architects and planners in particular, a fright-

ening amount of power, as they create a personal hypothesis in which others have to live and work.

9) Because each individual, whilst having the same fundamental mechanism, always has a slightly different relationship to the data, every human data bank must be different, and this must be true, irrespective of whether there are hereditary deep structures or not.

10) Repetitive information is parcelled up into pre-packaged blobs of information ready for re-use. Whilst this is necessary for survival, it is necessary to re-open these blobs from time to time to ensure that change has not made them incompatible with present needs. Not only is this necessary for individuals but also for sciences, institutions and religions, which often have these long outmoded standardized and formalized information blobs.

If we take this last proposition, it is only barely possible to imagine the traumatic 're-examining of the packages' during the Renaissance period when not only the concept of a round earth, the earth revolving around the sun, and other incredible feats of adjustment had to be absorbed, but such things as perspective representation entered their lives. These new ways of looking at things had a considerable effect on building thereafter, as we know.

Today we can only get some idea of how they felt as we try to accustom our minds to such ideas as infinite space within finite boundaries, black holes, negative mass, and other new mathematical concepts. It is equally certain that this change in our mental concepts will affect our attitudes to space and building, as the changes in concepts in the Renaissance changed theirs. For example, we have been inhibited for centuries in our way of thinking by using paper, which has restricted our thoughts to a two-dimensional hierarchical form. Advanced computer techniques have enabled the development of creative mathematics which permits three-dimensional explorations, which may yet have a dramatic effect on the way we use our minds. There now seems to be the possibility for us to start transferring mundane tasks to simple systems and machines, whilst opening up the possibility of developing personal creativity for everybody.

The alternative could be that we might be chained by the limitations of our tools. Existing tools such as drawing boards, tee squares and set squares, create an ever-increasing restriction on our thoughts, just as other tools have done in the past. Once designed, the tools restrict our activity. The way a motor car is designed prevents us from moving sideways. To take the point further, if we develop low level unimaginative computing systems, we shall later be inhibited by these systems. Furthermore, it is not only computers that can release or inhibit our progress in this way. It is for this reason that this chapter has dealt with the background information, because even mundane solutions to parts of the problem must be considered against a wider background if they are not to inhibit the whole.

The apparent finiteness of computing, when viewed superficially, has encouraged the continued beliefs in absolutism and reinforced the chains of Renaissance hierarchical thinking.

Chapter 2
DATA

Human beings, as data handling machines, are particularly good at handling very large quantities of data in a very imprecise way, but poor at repetitive and precise retrievals. Variety, for the sake of variety, is sometimes introduced in order to break the monotony of routine jobs. Sometimes this is even done where an effort could remove the job altogether. These deficiencies are a considerable handicap in a society which demands ever-increasing precision in all processes. Because the manual handling and filing of routine data is considered to be below the level of importance to management, it is often delegated to comparatively junior members of the staff, who quite reasonably, often organize the system for the ease of putting the information away, rather than for the real purpose, which is the easy retrieval of that information at a later date. Every office has a subject, or alphabetical system, but how many have one which arranges the retrieval according to the user's use, or the work function? How many systems work satisfactorily if the filing clerk is away?

It is without doubt an enormously difficult task to set up a good system, but it is surely unsatisfactory to relegate the life blood of an organization to relatively unskilled hands because it is a difficult, or unpleasant, task, as is surprisingly often done.

There have been some notable attempts to define the problem. Gordon (1966) proposed eight stages through which an office might proceed. He described them as follows:

'At stage one there was no library and architects kept their own collections of materials, probably inadequate, out-of-date and duplicating that kept by others. At stage two a move was made to set up a central library either by members of the office, or with part-time help, and at stage three with a full-time librarian. By then members of the office should have parted with most of their personal hoards but may well still have little faith in the library service, probably with good reason owing to its inability to give them the information they required quickly. By the time services had developed to a satisfactory level, stage four was reached; the office could then be said to have an efficient library system yielding information as requested.

If the library was to progress towards becoming a comprehensive information service it would then, at stage five, have begun to receive back from the office some tested information and to collect standard details. Very probably the library staff would have had to encourage members of the office to produce the kind of information needed on such matters as behaviour of methods of construction, components and materials in practice. When this experience was later fed back into the office for future projects a system preventing duplication of effort and error became established. Also at this stage the library staff started to move from single subject classifications to abstracting and giving information as well as presenting the enquirer with relevant documents. This may have involved some research. By stage six much fuller research was undertaken by the library, and a system of classification developed for information rather than data.

Few offices had yet reached stage seven. By then an effective feed-out service from the library was established. The library should keep closely in touch with the projects in the office and anticipate the information needs at the various stages of the designs. If on an early project records were kept of the information used, these could form the basis for future projects.

Finally, at stage eight, the librarian or technical information officer became in effect a member of the design team. He attended meetings, contributed to the discussion and produced the information he knew would be of use at that stage of the design. An architect on each new project was in constant touch with the library between meetings. Moreover, it was essential for the librarian to maintain a close and constant liaison with an architect, who would act as a sort of technical adviser to interpret other architects' requests to the library. By taking full advantage of all the library facilities in this way, at least time and effort could be saved and, further, standards of design and performance improved.'

The *Architects' Journal* gave a series of articles on the subject in 1968, and a survey of seventeen offices at that time did not suggest that offices had progressed very far up this scale, and there is little evidence of any very significant developments since that time.

So far, developments appear to have been somewhat limited, in spite of these works, and that which was commissioned by Government committees on data co-ordination. There is no doubt that the problem is formidable, but the one factor which tends to aggravate the problem is the inhibition of our two-dimensional thinking, which immediately drives us towards classical hierarchical structures to which complex coding systems are then applied. The reasons for this are no doubt historic. We grow up with hierarchical genealogical trees such as we find in history books, ignoring the fact that they are obviously severely limited, if not flagrantly distorted. To see a three dimensional genealogical tree, is to show up the deficiencies of such systems. (A three-dimensional structure of the Royal Family genealogical tree which was exhibited at Stratford-upon-Avon, well illustrated the limitations of the conventional approach). It is obvious that only direct descendants of one category (say son or daughter), can be shown. No connection between Harold and William I can be shown because the relationship is too complex.

The same thing happens when trying to set up two-dimensional simplistic coding structures.

Another influencing factor in the handling of data in the construction industry, appears to have been the attempt to relate hierarchical coding systems for the filing of books to construction. Whilst this has been useful to the industry in keeping the 'tide at bay', it must still have the inherent difficulties of the book referencing systems from which it developed, as well as the added ones relating to the industry.

These difficulties might briefly be listed as follows:

1. The impossibility of precisely fitting items into a necessarily imprecisely defined system. Whilst it is easy to find a place for say a door in the system, it becomes impossible to define the system adequately for the more obscure items. Therefore a lot of miscellanea finish up in ironmongery for example. (After all, what is ironmongery anyway?)
2. New subject areas are difficult to cope with.
3. The coding systems are often long and boring and sometimes more difficult to handle than the original data. This has no doubt been brought about by early contact with computer techniques which were unfortunately of the rather primitive kind. In other words, at the time when man was expected to handle the complicated codes rather than the machine.
4. No capacity for cross-searching.

This is not to decry the value of existing systems and the considerable contribution that they have made, but to illustrate a need to move on to a further stage. Because of the cost of reorganization, both in financial terms and in the disruption of the organization, data banks, whether human or mechanical, need to have a long-life structure. This makes it necessary to question whether there are other ways of handling the vast quantities of data which are probably unique to the industry, particularly as the development of the industry in the future will be held back more by the limitations of its information handling systems, than by any other single factor. If necessary, the subject area must be continuously explored to find solutions. It is unacceptable that almost all day-to-day building failures have been researched, and the results disseminated, but yet those results have not reached the next designer to make that same mistake. A re-examination of the basic problem might produce a possible direction, if not a final answer.

If one imagines any member of the building team, standing in the middle of all the documents necessary for him to carry out his contribution to the process, it would present a formidable array. The data for even quite a small job might easily fill a moderately sized room.

The architect for example, would need not only Building Regulations, Acts of Parliament, Codes of Practice, Technical data, etc, but also current research data on administration, social welfare, psychology, and so on and on. Even at the lowest level, the quantity would be too much for him to handle in the normal course of events, and so he will make guesses. It he were to be persistent in trying to do the job properly, he could try to find a piece of information by hunting systematically from one end of his heap of information to the other. This would soon prove to be an impossible system as it would be too time consuming. He would then set about dividing the pile into separate heaps, which would then become a classification system. He could do it by the size of book, sometimes seen in libraries, or by type, i.e. regulations, codes, etc. He would then, no doubt, break each heap down into further sub-heaps and so on. This is more-or-less how classification systems are devised, and immediately, one is trapped in the traditional Renaissance hierarchical structure which often creates more problems than it solves. Its attractiveness is greatest for the creator, who can set up increasingly precise sub-sections in the hierarchy, but unfortunately, the definitions already presuppose the answer to the problem. One can also immediately see the difficulties of cross-searching which lies at the basis

when the amount of data is small . . . . .

. . . . . this can easily be searched.
But, as it increases . . . . .

. . . . . it becomes necessary to group data
in some way to reduce area of search.

Figure 6

of all creative work. Most creative work depends upon using items in differing contexts from those in which they would normally be expected to be seen, but hierarchical classification systems have to file items under classes of components even though, for example, patent roof-glazing is sometimes used as a wall, and flooring materials are sometimes put on walls, and so on. The first time this is done, the item would not be found in the traditional classifications, and therefore new ideas depend upon human memory again.

An alternative way would be for him to think that the data he requires exists only because he himself exists as a human being. If human beings didn't exist, and the world was inhabited by, say, animals alone, there would be no door handles, no doors, nor even the regulations and codes relating to us. Even when we collect information on animals, it is from our own viewpoint as human beings, and not from the viewpoint of the animals. Therefore it might

whilst data changes . . . . man himself does not change

Figure 7

be reasonable to assume that we could set up a system relating to human needs and activities.

From this it can be deduced that these basic activities do not change, because man, as we have seen, does not change. It is only the means by which we achieve the activities that change. This leads to the first hopeful sign

31

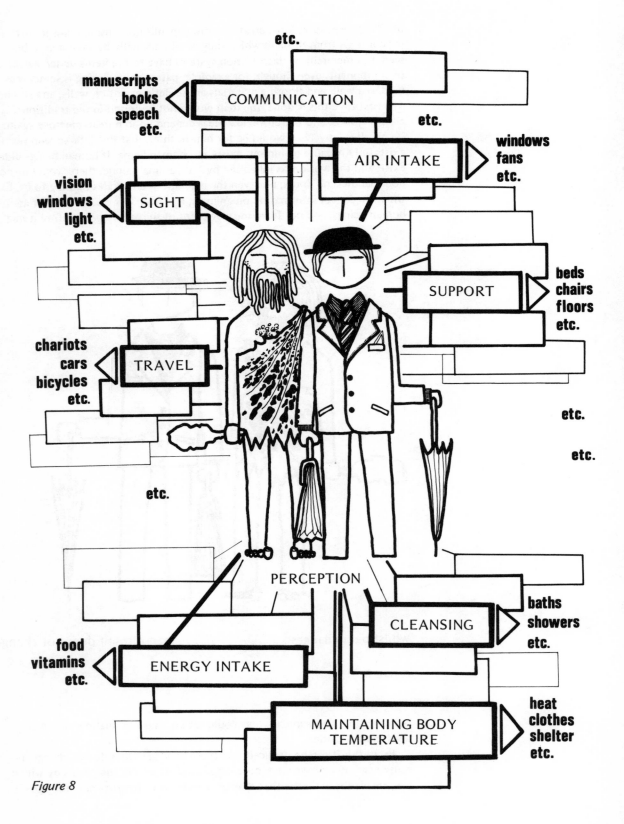

etc.

manuscripts
books
speech
etc.

COMMUNICATION

etc.

AIR INTAKE

windows
fans
etc.

vision
windows
light
etc.

SIGHT

beds
chairs
floors
etc.

SUPPORT

chariots
cars
bicycles
etc.

TRAVEL

etc.

etc.

etc.

PERCEPTION

CLEANSING

baths
showers
etc.

food
vitamins
etc.

ENERGY INTAKE

heat
clothes
shelter
etc.

MAINTAINING BODY
TEMPERATURE

Figure 8

that these activities could form the basis of a long lasting structure (Figure 8).

To take a single example. The transportation needs of man throughout the ages has not been the chariot, or the bicycle, or the car, or the aeroplane, but it has always been, and will always be, a function of travelling between one place and another. If we classified our systems on any of the types of transport, we should have to restructure the system every time a new invention was made. But if we file our information as a basic human function, and classify an object's ability to satisfy that function, then we would have a system which would last for as long as man remained on the planet. Figure 9 illustrates the point in a very simple way.

The other interesting aspect is that it is self-coding. It will be noticed that each item fulfils the functions differently, and the indication of this creates a coding structure easily recognized, not only by a computer but by any edge punched card system. (The ticks and crosses represent the code).

functions

travel 'a to b'	✔	✔	✔	✔
exercise	✔	✔	✘	✘
protection from the weather	✘	✘	✔	✔
confined to hard surface	✘	✔	✔	✘

Figure 9

To summarize the advantages so far:

1. It is not time-dependent. If a system of this sort had been set up by the Romans for instance, who might have input walking, and riding, it would still be relevant today for inserting the present modes of travel which are fulfilling the same functions of moving from A to B.

2. A search can be made for the solution most relevant to the problem — cross-searching. Most existing systems assume that the solution to the problem is known when the search is started, but this pre-knowledge is not always available, nor even desirable, because this can cause many of the

33

defective choices made. The danger is obvious. In an environment of expanding data, the searcher only seeks that which he already knows exist, or at least limits his search to the appropriate classification; but obviously this is totally inhibiting. In the proposed system, the searcher can specify the functions, and the degree to which he wishes them to be fulfilled, and then anything which satisfies these requirements will be offered to him.

3. A search can be made by several different approaches. For example, by function, by name or by description.

4. The user doesn't need to know, or to remember, any code at all.

All of this may be illustrated in a simple form, namely the selection of a motor car. There are at present more than six hundred different makes and types of motor car available on the British market alone. No one choosing a car would work their way through each one irrespective of price, type, etc. until he came to one which fulfilled his need. He would go about it in the same way as the system just described, (i.e. by selecting criteria) and in order to help him, the proposed system could be put into operation. In fact, just such a system was demonstrated at the R.I.B.A., and other similar examples have been shown at Motor Shows over the last few years.

Firstly, a card for each car type is completed, stating its ability to fulfil basic criteria.

Travel

max speed - in miles per hour
cost in use - in pence per mile
carrying load - in kilograms
mode - land, sea, air
UUUUU
WW
yyyyy
zzzzzzz
KLLLLLL
JJJKKKKK
UUUUU
FFFFFFFGGGG
ZZZZ

		scales of values											
		0	1	2	3	4	5	6	7	8	9	
speed	A				X							mph
cost	B							X				ppmile
load	C					X						kg
mode	D				X							
UUUUU	E			X								&
WWW	F							X				££
yyy	G									X		$
ZZZZ	H								X			$¢
KLLLL	I		X									??
JKKKK	J											&
UUUUU	K											¢
FFFGGG	L											$
ZZZ	M											$

IMPLIED CODE: A3, B7, C5, D4, E2, F6, ETC.

Figure 10

These criteria would be such things as number of seats, petrol consumption under given condition, cruising speed, cost range, etc. In other words, the normal factors included in any road test report, which of course makes the input of data very simple.

The selector or user now specifies his need, i.e. 4 seater, petrol consumption of not less than 30 mpg, cost range, etc. It is plain to see that the cards which match his need are the cars for him to consider, and the remainder he need not bother with, as they do not fulfil his needs.

The sortation of these cards may be made in a variety of ways depending upon the scale of the problem. One way is to use edge punch cards where the edges of the data cards have holes and slots. When inserting needles into the appropriate criteria, the cards which are not applicable will have holes, and will therefore be held, but the cards which do satisfy the appropriate criteria will have the holes turned into slots by a simple machine, and will therefore allow the suitable cards to drop from the pack. This system can be seen in many estate agents' offices where the clients' needs are matched to the houses on offer.

This method, of course, is satisfactory for small quantities of data, but as the volume increases another method of processing must be adopted, and so a computer is used, which can not only process the information in a similar way, but also assist in its selection.

In the edge punch card system described, all cards have an equal weighting, so that a near miss on an important criterion is left out, but a hit on a low criterion item is retained. By providing an opportunity for the selector to give preferential loading to various items, the process can be further sophisticated. Barbour Index have operated trials in several offices using this approach for bricks and sanitary fittings. It has been proved beyond doubt that the system works. It might be argued that it would be difficult to establish the criteria required for the whole building industry, but fortunately this work has already largely been done. In 1964, the Conseil International du Bâtiment produced a report called 'A master list of properties for building materials and products'. This provided a comprehensive set of headings or criteria for collecting information on properties, and which was found to be ideal for the preparation of product data sheets along the lines described above, and its effect can be seen in many technical brochures.

In 1972 they issued a new edition called 'The CIB MASTER LISTS for structuring documents relating to buildings, building elements, components, materials and services'. Two things are highlighted by these two reports. An examination of the two lists shows that the original basic list was remarkably pure, proving that long lasting criteria are possible. The other thing that the production of the new edition for structuring documents suggests, is that the original edition was not only good, but had shown a new potential.

There is now no doubt that the whole mass of building materials and components could be filed in the manner described, and that the selector could be provided with all relevant solutions, merely by making an enquiry on the level of criteria by which he will make judgements. These criteria will not only include the physical attributes of the material or component which immediately reduces risks of failures, but can also include colour, shape and other more aesthetic judgements and can even be automatically related to microfilm pictures or existing brochures. This after all is the normal way one would expect to make selections in one's own mind, as the motor car example shows. Furthermore, there are no hierarchies, for one in effect creates a new personal hierarchy for every given situation, again, much as the mind appears to work.

This provides the basis of a data bank which will primarily offer to the selector those items which are suitable for the task — this in itself must be a big step forward. In addition, it provides a capability for cross-searching. Instead of searching for, say, 'Windows', as in most systems one can search for items in the bank which one 'Can see through', and 'Weatherproof', etc. thereby enabling the creative designer to be offered rooflights for a wall, for example. This may not at first sight appear to be an important factor, but it must be remembered that a large number of new materials and components are reaching the market which cannot possibly be assimilated or evaluated by the design team. The system also allows of course, for products to be selected by criteria, and in addition, if one knows the item to be chosen, it can be selected by name of product or name of manufacturer. This shows the possibility for a data bank of products which could be ageless and with no need for laborious coding structures.

Other needs for the data bank must now be explored, but before this

A   SITE

B   STRUCTURAL   SUPPORT

C   VERTICAL   ENVELOPE

D   SPACE   DIVIDER

E   BASE   PLATFORM

F   INTERMEDIATE   PLATFORM

G   HORIZONTAL   ENVELOPE

H   VERTICAL   CIRCULATION

I   ENVIRONMENTAL   CONTROL

J   SERVICING

K   EXTERNAL   ENVIRONMENT

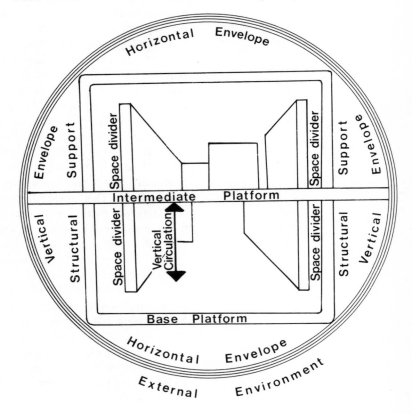

Figure 11

can be done, the basic functional needs of a building must be established against which these basic criteria will be judged.

The following classification of these functions is only for the purpose of description, and not to be considered as mutually exclusive functions.

Figure 11 illustrates these basic functions in a simple form to act as a sort of purgative. To rid the classification system of names which imply decisions,

a	SITE	Clearance of site, demolition of Existing Structures and other works necessary to return site to normal conditions. Drains and services up to building and boundary definitions.
B	STRUCTURAL SUPPORT	Support structure and its normal foundations.
C	VERTICAL ENVELOPE	Encloses structure and protects from elements (rain, wind, sun, cold, etc.)
D	SPACE DIVIDER	Divides spaces vertically to give visual and oral privacy. (Can be INTERNAL OR EXTERNAL)
e	BASE PLATFORM	Lowest floor level.
F	INTERMEDIATE PLATFORM	Divides space horizontally.
G	HORIZONTAL ENVELOPE	Protects from elements horizontally and encloses structure at roof level.
H	VERTICAL CIRCULATION	Provides access between horizontal surfaces at different levels.
i	ENVIRONMENTAL CONTROL	Modifies internal environment and provides conditions suitable for human habitation.
J	SERVICING	Provides PHYSICAL properties required by occupants of structure.
K	EXTERNAL ENVIRONMENT	Provides visual and physical amenities.

Figure 12

these zones are described in terms of the functions they are required to fulfil, rather than the names of the components such as 'windows' and 'walls' which are already preselective by their description. One possible description of the functions of building is as follows, and will suffice for a hypothesis (Figure 12).

These descriptions are very sparse, because the object is to establish a hypothesis upon which the data base can be developed, and in any case, this subject area has been more than adequately covered in the *Architects' Journal* Handbook for Building Enclosure.

It can be seen from these listed functions that there are three major deficiencies in the data bank so far proposed. They are, means of filing and retrieving site information, an activity file, and meteorological details, all of which are needed to be known before the selection criteria for most functions can be established.

To deal with the latter first:

If an ideal weather-controlled climate, adjusted to man's bodily needs, were possible, it may not even be necessary to have a building at all. As this is not possible, the major part of a building's function is as a climate modifier, and the degree of modification must depend upon the building's location from a human point of view. Clearly the wind forces are likely to be more severe in the Shetland Isles than in the Mediterranean area. Similarly, temperature modification, rainfall run-off and so on, are dependent upon the building's location within a meteorological environment. This data has been available for a long time, but because of the difficulty of handling it amongst all the other information, it has led to averaging and rough guesswork being used instead. For example, the long and tedious task of calculating 2 per cent daylight factors, as required at one time by the Department of Education and Science, led Architects to over-glaze to be on the safe side, rather than go through the complications of the calculations with its consequent disastrous effect upon energy consumption and human environment as seen today in hindsight. Rough and ready rules for glazing established themselves as a fashion for large windows. Only the energy crisis brought home the troubles which this approach obviously carried in its wake. But with a proper meteorological base, the location of a site would immediately bring forward in the data base all the relevant criteria for subsequent processing.

The next deficiency is that of activities. If it were possible to provide a basic list of human activities, these could be compared with the environment in which they are to take place, and from these, building shape and materials can be developed. For example, the interaction between climate and activity, means that coffee will be drunk in open air cafes in Mediterranean climates, but almost never in northerly climates.

At first sight, the work on ergonomics might suggest that the range of human activities would be too vast to contemplate holding in one data base, but a closer examination suggests that the activities of man are, just as one found with the functions of building, quite limited. It is the variety of ways in which they are used which gives the appearance of a great range. For instance, an average man aged 40 years, sitting at a desk, writing has the same needs whether he be a doctor, patient, teacher, student and so on (Figure 13).

Typical actions are as follows:

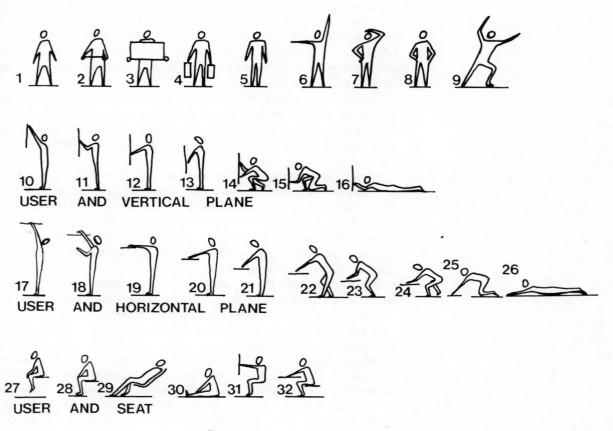

Figure 13

01 — Walk
02 — Walk and carry 0.600 m wide object with 2 hands
03 — Walk and carry 1.200 m wide object with 2 hands
04 — Walk and carry object in either hand
05 — Stand
06 — Stand and reach (arms fully extended)
07 — Stand and reach (arms bent)
08 — Lie
09 — Lie and stretch
10 — Stand and work at vertical surface (above head level)
11 — Stand and work at vertical surface (eye level)
12 — Stand and work at vertical suf ace (shoulder level)
13 — Stand and work at vertical surface (waist level)
14 — Crouch at vertical surface
15 — Kneel at vertical surface
16 — Lie at vertical surface
17 — Stand and work at horizontal surface (over head)
18 — Stand and work at horizontal surface (above head level)
19 — Stand and work at horizontal surface (eye level)

20 — Stand and work at horizontal surface (shoulder level)
21 — Stand and work at horizontal surface (waist level)
22 — Stand and work at horizontal surface (thigh level)
23 — Bend and work at horizontal surface (knee high)
24 — Crouch and work at horizontal surface
25 — Kneel and work at horizontal surface
26 — Lie and work at horizontal surface
27 — Sit on high chair
28 — Sit on upright chair
29 — Sit on easy chair
30 — Sit on floor
31 — Sit and work at vertical surface
32 — Sit and work at horizontal surface.

The activities and their environmental requirements will vary with age, and therefore the human needs for various activities must be held for all age ranges because the air temperature needs of old people, for example, is different from those of young people, and so on. These needs will include air temperature, humidity levels, aural ranges and all other basic human needs and characteristics which can be held on simple matrix files. The next chapter will explain how these might be used.

Furniture and equipment to suit these activities can be held in the same matrix enquiry form already described, for selection by criteria which in turn are selected from the activity needs. In other words the activity and the selected person combine to give the criteria for selection of furniture and equipment.

It must be emphasized that the use of the data bank must be flexible, and leave the decisions to the users even though its form is based on the CIB Master Lists. *It is a tool to be used.* For example, the aural range shown in the files may indicate that the level of sound required in a discothéque exceeds safe levels, but it is the selector who must make the judgement. At least he is consciously overriding known criterion; as opposed to making decisions, as too often at present, in ignorance.

Now there remains the problem of building up data upon the selected site. The climatic details are known, but the topological and other characteristics are, as yet, not covered. In a normal manual operation, the site is surveyed to establish the different levels on a grid basis, and descriptions and measurements of boundaries and other details are recorded, according to the individual surveyor's persuasion. This involves reducing the levels to establish the site configuration, calculations for the establishment of the shape of the site, and the interpretation of notes and symbols to enable the location and description of site details, such as trees.

But it is now possible to put the original site data into a computer, so that it can not only carry out the routine calculations, but also produce a drawing with all relevant information.

Most important of all, not only can levels and contours of the site and shape of the land be held in the machine, but by the use of a standardized range of symbols of the type used on ordnance survey sheets, all the other site details can also be stored and held for future uses. A typical range of symbols is given in Figure 14.

Before moving on to the communication flow and the processing of data, it would be useful to summarize the data now held in the data bank, whether this be at national, group, or individual level.

1. A store of known materials and components, which can be selected by the criteria for which they will be needed to satisfy a building function.
2. A store of human activities and human needs, on an age/sex basis, which will provide spatial information as well as environmental criteria.
3. A store of furniture and equipment, which can be selected on the basis of criteria, but which are also related to the file on human activities and needs.
4. Meteorological and other environmental data on a national or local basis.
5. Site details on a local basis.

LAMPOST	CP CESS PIT	REFERENCE OBJECT	— —IL IMPROVE-MENT LINE
WATER TAP	SK SOAKAWAY	— F — FOUL DRAIN	ROAD
TELEGRAPH POLE	T TELEPHONE BOX	— S — STORMWATER DRAIN	------ FOOTPATH
FH FIRE HYDRANT	▥ ROAD GULLEY	— T — TELEPHONE WIRE	∨∨∨ HEDGES
▫ POST	T H TRIAL HOLE	— W — WATER MAIN	—+—+— FENCES
PYLON	⬡ TREE	— E — ELECTRIC MAIN	STREAM/ DITCH
□ MANHOLE F - FOUL S - STORM WATER	BM BENCH MARK	— G — GAS MAIN	xxxxxxxx UNDER-GROWTH
GATE GATE	TBM TEMPORARY BENCHMARK	— —BL BUILDING LINE	✳ SPECIAL ITEM
SP SERVICE PIT	✛ SPOT HEIGHT	— —FL FLOOD LINE	

Figure 14

The value of such a data bank can hardly be disputed. The criteria are known to exist, but the possibility of obtaining the data may be questioned. There is no doubt from experience already gained, that manufacturers and suppliers would supply the criteria for their products, once these have been established. They already supply much of the information, but unfortunately, too often in an incompatible form, because there is no direction. If direction were given using the CIB Master Lists, and these were related to Agrément Certificates, the selector would be in a much better position to choose the product most suitable for his needs. Even shape can be included in this selection criteria. This would quickly supply the information for categories 1 and 3. The information for items 2 and 4 is already available in many disparate areas, and only needs collating and organizing. Item 5 is already being dealt with on an *ad hoc* basis, and only regularization of approach is needed. This would provide a good data base for the construction industry, and if a similar approach were adopted by other industries and professions it would obviously be possible, in the course of time, for other areas of knowledge about human needs, activities and manufactures to be searched in exactly the same way. If it is assumed that the data base has been set up according to these criteria, the next problem is to consider possible mechanisms for manipulating the data to enable the design team to make decisions, not on the basis of single optimum choices even if they are optima, but on the basis of choice through multiple interactive matrices.

Chapter 3
INFORMATION FLOW

Once general policy has been settled on whether or not to build, the first requirements of both client and designers is a comprehensive brief and details of the site location. The questions and answers around which the brief is built up is in the order of where; who; how many; what do they do and when; and these can lead to an examination of needs in terms of activities, and the interrelationship of activities. Sometimes this analysis is shortcut by making assumptions on rooms, or even groups of rooms. This of course can, and has been, taken to the extreme of using standard plans, but to set up an information flow system on this basis, would be a disastrous thing, as it would prejudice the future. To see the dangers, one only has to consider how a data base and information flow, based on rooms or part plans, would have completely prevented the creation of Bürolandschaft, or open plan offices. This example should be sufficient to show how the collection of basic data must not be at such a high level that it will inhibit the future.

To ensure a proper analysis of user needs, the designer must go to the basic activities of the users, and at once, he is involved in complex ranges of associations, of activity data and user requirements interacting with the environment in which the activities will be carried out. It is from this mass of interrelated data that he tries to devise optimum solutions. As we have seen, there cannot be an optimum in absolute terms, but only a solution which gives the greatest cost benefit at that moment. Whilst a supply of good information doesn't guarantee a good creative synthesis, it is clear that a good solution cannot be obtained in ignorance. Ideally the synthesis or creative leap would need almost simultaneous examination and digestion of all the facts impinging on each other at any one time, but this is quite impossible, because the scale of data required is too great for any single brain to hold. For this reason, the design process is stretched out into a series of sub-problems. Jones (1970) has summarized the problem very clearly.

'Why are the new kinds of complexity beyond the scope of the traditional design process?

We have seen that the main difficulty in any form of designing is that of coping with the complexity of a huge search space filled with millions of alternative combinations of possible sub-components. We have also seen that this otherwise unmanageable variety is dealt with traditionally by concentrating on one sub-problem at a time. This

can be done only if most of the combinations of sub-components
are eliminated by confining the investigation to a single tentative set
of sub-components whose interrelationships can be perceived and
manipulated on a scale drawing. The critical stage in this process is
not the mutual adjustment of sub-components until they fit each
other but the creative leap by which the brain, of a sufficiently
informed and sufficiently uninhibited person, can select a promising
set of sub-components in the first place. This works well at the
level of products and components, but seems most unlikely to work
when the levels of systems and communities are included as well.
The reasons for the difficulty at higher level can be summarised as
follows:

1. Without something equivalent to a drawing (in which to store,
   and to manipulate, the relationships between products) the
   system designer is not free to concentrate upon one bit of the
   problem at a time and he has no medium in which to communicate the essence of the mental imagery with which he could
   conceive of a tentative solution which would enable him to
   drastically shorten his search. To stick to the traditional use of
   drawings of products as the stable elements in a creative search
   process is, of course, to utterly inhibit innovation at the systems
   level.
2. Without some systems equivalent of the well-informed and
   uninhibited brain-and-pencil of a skilled designer there is no
   means of making the very rapid judgements of the feasibility of
   critical details that makes possible the leap of insight that turns
   an overcomplicated problem into one that is simple enough to
   solve by attending to the sub-problems in sequence rather than
   simultaneously. Unfortunately the information necessary to
   assess the feasibility of a new system proposal is scattered among
   many brains and many publications and some of it may have to
   be discovered by new research.
3. Many of the people who carry in their experience the pieces of
   information upon which the designing of a new system depends,
   have vested interests in rejecting anything but small departures
   from the *status quo* and are likely to make biased judgements
   upon the long term merits or demerits of major changes.
4. The selection of simplifying proposals that are sufficiently precise
   to permit detailed exploration of feasibility involves the exercise
   of value judgements that, at the systems level, are vital to the
   community interests. It is essential if such judgements are to be
   effective in removing major socio-technical evils, that they are
   compatible with all the social, economic, technical data that is
   needed to predict detailed feasibility at all four levels in the
   hierarchy of communities, systems, products and components.'

If the information which has to be analysed is small enough to be held
and mulled over in one human brain, then one synthesis or creative leap is
possible. But when the size of the problem increases, the information to

be analysed increases, and because it cannot be mulled over in one brain session, it is broken down into sub-solutions, and when the problem becomes even larger, other brains are brought in to share the sub-problems, and maybe even further sub-problems are created. Apart from the gradual specialization of the parts, and the problems that that brings, it is clear that optimal solution of sub-problems do not necessarily make optimal solutions to a main problem. This then causes an iterative process to be established — a process which at best extends the design time, and at worst causes confusion within the team.

Once this iterative approach has to take place, the final synthesis is slowed down, and when the sub-problems are handled by specialists far away from the person making the major synthesis, this iterative process grows at an alarming rate, because each is developing parts of a proposal independently and very often divergently, which cause a need for constant reconsultation. It is clear then, that the simplest way to achieve large solutions is to:

(a) Refine the data so that extraneous information is discarded.
(b) When specialists are required in order that a problem can be sub-divided, the lines of communication must be kept as short as possible.

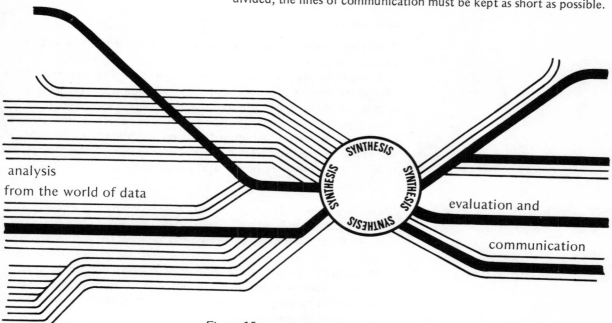

analysis
from the world of data

evaluation and

communication

Figure 15

The establishment of a data base as described in Chapter 2, can help this problem of information flow for analysis, synthesis, and evaluation.

There are two main cycles of information flow in the design and construction process. The first is the flow of information based upon data collection and analysis, which leads up to the design hypothesis and its subsequent testing and evaluation. The second is the information flow emanating from the design decisions which enable construction to be carried out (Figure 15).

But whilst this information flow falls into these two neat categories, it is essential that both are integrated into a complete and logical whole, because the changes that have already happened have stripped away the latent information which made the old system work. The traditional system is represented by the R.I.B.A. plan of work, which has provided the industry with an excellent basis upon which to co-ordinate the information flow, but this is an administrative plan as opposed to a functional plan, and it is worth considering the alternative.

INFORMATION: Input/Data Store/Output
DESIGN: Analysis/Synthesis/Evaluation
COMMUNICATION: Constructional
                      Financial
CONSTRUCTION: Construction Management
               Financial Management
MAINTENANCE AND CONTROL

The analysis of each of these functions is now considered in more detail:

Information

Before any creative decision can take place, there must be access to an adequate supply of information.

It is easy to take for granted the large data base which we carry around with us and which has been built up during a lifetime, and therefore it is as well to remember, that had any of us been kept in a dark box from birth, deprived of all sensory data, we would not be able to make any creative act, as there would be no data upon which to make a hypothesis. Therefore, we must assume that the richer the data; the richer the possible solution. There are three aspects of INFORMATION:

Input: This is the extension of our own sensory inputs into specialized forms. For example, primitive man would look around him to see the problems of the site upon which he was to build. Today, this would be an input of data by a surveyor. It is therefore important to reconsider the input of data, not just in terms of filing clerks, but as that whole range of expertise including researchers, journalists, surveyors and so on, who are building up the data bank in order that the analysis of data may be of the highest order.

Data Store: This is the structure which has to be designed to suit the needs of each particular part of the building team, desirably on the principles proposed in Chapter 3. It is the responsibility of the Data Store to ascertain the future needs of Design and other subsequent stages in the process, and set Input the task of providing the data. Data Store then files the information in the most efficient way, so that output becomes a more or less mechanical operation. It is clear that this is a most important part of the organization as it is a direct supplement for the brain. The storage of data will range from conventional filing systems and books, through systems such as edge punch cards, to the most sophisticated computer systems.

Output: This can be either manual, or mechanical, or both, and if the data store is properly organized, becomes just a physical translation of information from the store to the user.

Design

The flow of information from INFORMATION, gives the opportunity for analysis of the data to be followed by a synthesis, and then evaluation.
   The synthesis, or creative leap, is outside the scope of this book for reasons already given, but assuming that the data and its analysis is good, then the evaluation and testing of the design hypothesis should be good. Against this background, analytical and evaluative processes can be developed which will not hinder or restrict, but only help the human brain to carry out the synthesis of the many components of the design.

Communication

The communication of the design to the Constructor has become confused in the last hundred years or so, and has often led to systems where instructions for the work required to be done, and the financial control have become intertwined, very often to the detriment of both. For this reason, these two aspects of communicating design will be kept separate in this analysis. In the purest sense, the building team on site, only require instructions to carry out the requirements of the design. The financial agreement and control is another process which can be handled separately.

Construction

The information which the constructor uses for both construction management and financial management has emanated from the design process, and is part of a continuous flow which will eventually provide further data for the data store.

Maintenance – Control

Much of the information generated during design is often discarded, when it could be usefully employed at this stage. This is not a separate activity, but a part of the information flow.

   The establishment of functional groupings as part of a logical progression can have an effect on the management system, and this will gradually be developed. Areas of uncertainty in the pre-design stage are gradually reduced as the process moves from the general to the particular, and ultimately to the precise, in each area of choice – selection – decision.

The flow of information is continuous and spiral like in form, making it impossible to find a true beginning. Therefore the flow will be cut, and the examination started from the input of data. The flow is spiral like rather than cyclical, because new knowledge changes the data base from which the next process begins.

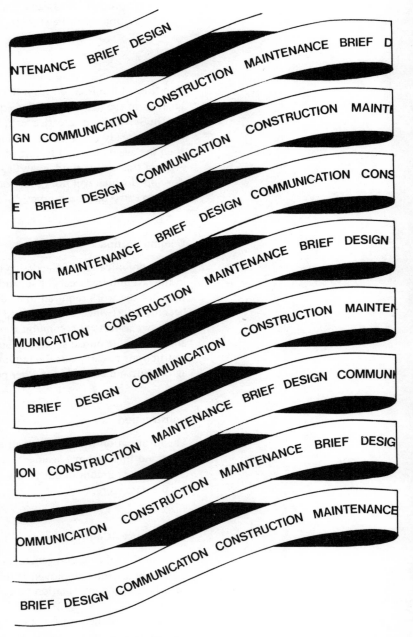

Figure 16

Apart from the continual input of new knowledge, the experience gained through construction and maintenance enhances the information contained in the data base, so that the next project starts from a slightly different position.

Given the data base proposed, it is worth examining possible ways in which this can give direct assistance to the design team in building projects.

1. The site plan with all its relevant details cannot only be retrieved, but there is the opportunity for using manipulative systems such as the MOSS system — A Modelling System of Highway Design and related Disciplines — Craine, Houlton and Malcomson (1974). They explain its development as follows,

> 'From the experience gained in the development and use of what may be called "conventional" highway design programs. . . it was decided to investigate the complete process of computer aided highway engineering with a view to producing a single computer system which would permit the design of all highway geometry and facilitate the interaction between man and machine.
>
> Such a system would have to replace the many different and questionably adequate suites of programs hitherto available and also be sufficiently flexible to cope with alterations and extensions to the design technique. When such a generalization of approach is required it is almost always achieved by returning to the basic principles of the application and MOSS is no exception'.

Again the point is made that one needs to return to basic principles when developing systems for a generalized approach.

> 'A major concern in new developments at the present time is the environmental impact. MOSS provides basic environmental options for noise and visual intrusion as well as those. . . for plotting isometric and perspective views.
>
> For route location investigations, each hamlet, estate, or other development is defined with parameters such as population, number of hereditaments, as well as its geocode position, and an index for noise prediction and visual intrusion is aggregated for the given new route. By comparing routes and their associated indices, the environmental effects of the new works can be minimized.
>
> The affected area around a route or development can be interrogated and MOSS will output noise contours at given predicted decibel levels. It will also show the limit of visual contact with the boundary of the scheme allowing overall visual intrusion to be assessed from one diagram.
>
> This type of exercise can be used to determine the effect of the creation of new industrial land use on its surroundings, and with new town expansion studies MOSS should provide extremely good assessments of the environmental intrusion of industry, roads etc.'

2. Input of numbers of users, their types and activities into other programs can provide alternative sortations of relationships. For example the noisy and quiet activities can be sorted, or those needing daylight or not needing daylight can be sorted. As Broadbent (1973) says:

'There are two reasons. . . for placing an activity in a particular position — or rather, two major reasons, each with many ramifications. The first of these is environmental; as a simple instance of this, other things being equal, one would not place an activity which needed quiet on the noisy side of the building. The other reasons are concerned with relationships between activities, and these two can be subdivided into environmental, functional and circulatory. . .

At this stage we cannot consider all the environmental implications because much will depend on the environment into which we shall be building. . . Suffice it to say. . . that as part of the process we shall define the block of space available for building into, in such a way that it will be possible to allocate positions, for certain critical activities at least. In order to do that, we may need to define a hierarchy of activities, to order them according to some system, in order of importance so that when activities compete for space, as inevitably they will, we shall know how to order their priorities.

Sometimes the hierarchy will be presented to us by the client; it may be the only aspect of the briefing which really concerns him. The difficulty is that any such statement of hierarchy might raise our egalitarian blood. If we modify Le Corbusier's view and admit, at least, that all men have similar organisms, then their needs of the environment, if they are to be comfortable, will be similar if not identical. Clearly, in any building some parts of three-dimensional space will be inherently more comfortable than others; how shall we allocate them? We might take a utilitarian view that our prime concern is the greatest happiness for the greatest number of people.

. . . certain techniques from decision-making will help us specifically with this class of problem. They can take into account not only the hard financial facts of the case, but people's values as well, and we can apply them with any degree of precision. Suppose, for instance, we take the few environmental requirements which have been shown to influence the position of an activity in the building. As part of our activity brief, we allocated a subjective impression of importance to each of these. Thus for one activity we might have allocated 'quiet location' as the most important factor of all, whilst another might need strict north light.'

There are obviously many possible permutations to meet these conditions. If environmental, social or financial criteria have been ordered into an initial grouping of activities the next stage of analysis can begin. They can be grouped into sets and subsets, possibly using Venn diagrams for preparing a different grouping for each environmental condition. As before, the analysis can be undertaken manually, mechanically, or by computer, but in each case, a rich pattern of interconnexions between activities must be built up. The crudest, and among the most effective tools for use at this point, are the interaction chart, in one of its many forms, the flow chart, and the random connexions diagram (Figure 17).

All of that described by Broadbent can be carried out within the machine, ready for analysis or evaluation, as the case may be.

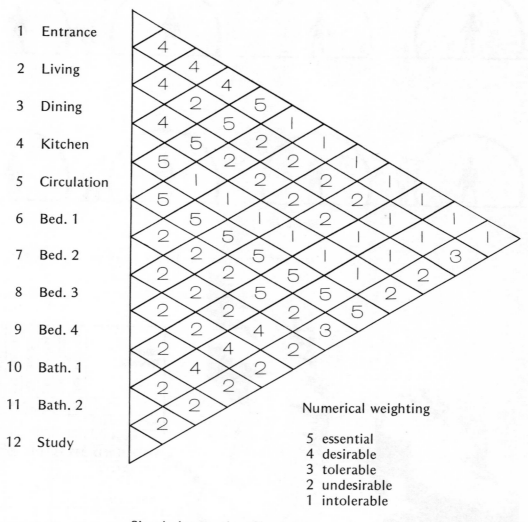

1 Entrance

2 Living

3 Dining

4 Kitchen

5 Circulation

6 Bed. 1

7 Bed. 2

8 Bed. 3

9 Bed. 4

10 Bath. 1

11 Bath. 2

12 Study

Numerical weighting

5 essential
4 desirable
3 tolerable
2 undesirable
1 intolerable

Simple Interaction Chart

Figure 17

3. Location of site will retrieve all climatic data relevant to the proposed design.

With this potential retrieval of background information, the process up to the stage of the design hypothesis could be described in simple diagrammatic form as follows.

Activities can therefore be examined against climatic conditions.

Figure 18

Data base is searched for climatic data appropriate to that location.

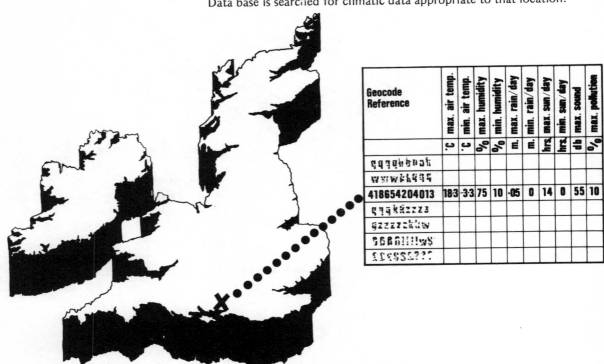

Geocode Reference	°C max. air temp.	°C min. air temp.	% max. humidity	% min. humidity	m. max. rain/day	m. min. rain/day	hrs. max. sun/day	hrs. min. sun/day	db max. sound	% max. pollution
ꞔꞔꞵꞵꞵꞵꞵꞵ										
ꜽꜽꝒꝒꝀꝀꝀꝀ										
418654204013	**18·3**	**-3·3**	**75**	**10**	**·05**	**0**	**14**	**0**	**55**	**10**
ꞔꞔꝀꝁꝈꝈꝈꝈ										
ꝀꝈꝈꝈꝈꝀꝁꝁ										
ꝒꝀꝀꝀꝒꝒꝒꝒ										
ꝈꝈꝈꝈꝈꝈꝈꝈ										

Figure 19

Data base is informed of numbers of users and their activities which initiates search of data base for information on the basis of activity, age,

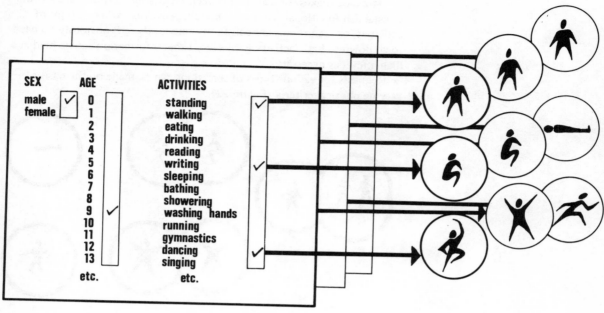

Figure 20

and sex, which can also activate equipment data when necessary.

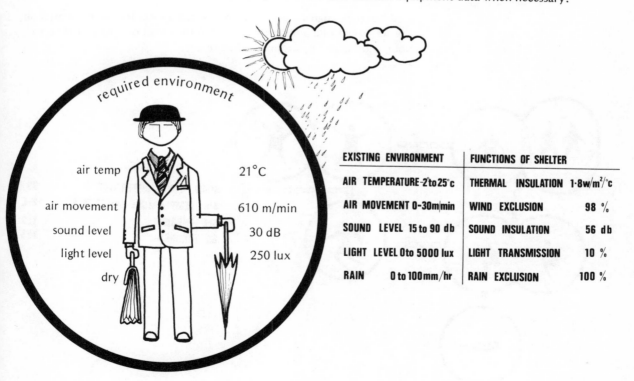

EXISTING ENVIRONMENT	FUNCTIONS OF SHELTER	
AIR TEMPERATURE -2°to 25°c	THERMAL INSULATION	1·8w/m²/°c
AIR MOVEMENT 0-30m/min	WIND EXCLUSION	98 %
SOUND LEVEL 15 to 90 db	SOUND INSULATION	56 db
LIGHT LEVEL 0 to 5000 lux	LIGHT TRANSMISSION	10 %
RAIN 0 to 100mm/hr	RAIN EXCLUSION	100 %

required environment

air temp	21°C
air movement	610 m/min
sound level	30 dB
light level	250 lux
dry	

Figure 21

Data base makes comparison between activity needs and local conditions to establish functional criteria for building envelope. Where groups of activities, or even rooms are constantly reused, there is obviously no need to go down to basic activity level every time. Information can be held at a higher level as necessary.

Requests for various types of sortations can be made on the basis of varying physical criteria (Figure 22).

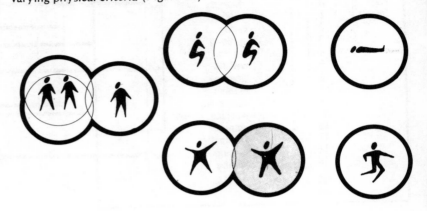

Figure 22

After the designer has selected or created a sortation, which is after all, the equivalent of a bubble diagram, then the effect of each activity area upon another can be examined (Figure 23).

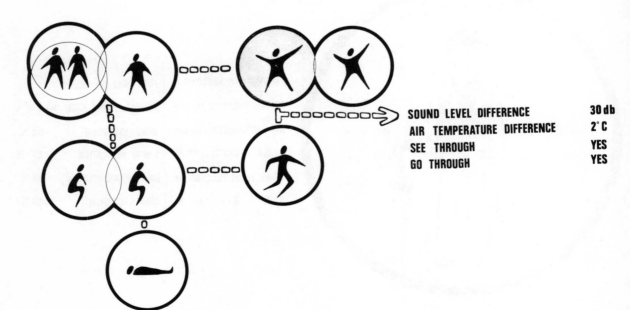

SOUND LEVEL DIFFERENCE   **30 db**
AIR TEMPERATURE DIFFERENCE   **2° C**
SEE THROUGH   **YES**
GO THROUGH   **YES**

Figure 23

Obviously a noisy area adjoining a quiet area (both deducible from the activity data), creates a need for sound insulation, but equally obviously this depends upon the degree of proximity. As the two areas are moved closer together, the computer is able to establish the increasing sound insulation needs of a space divider. Similarly, with any other criteria (Figure 24).

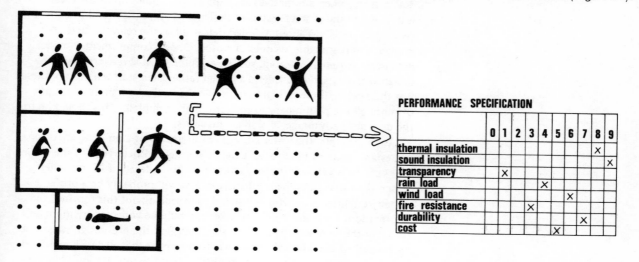

PERFORMANCE SPECIFICATION	0	1	2	3	4	5	6	7	8	9
thermal insulation									x	
sound insulation										x
transparency		x								
rain load					x					
wind load							x			
fire resistance					x					
durability								x		
cost						x				

Figure 24

Three-dimensional shapes can now be created, and because the relationship between activities and their relationship to the climatic conditions, create the criteria by which materials and components are selected, it is simple for the computer to make its own search of the data base because it has been constructed on the basis of these same criteria. This enables it to find appropriate materials and components for selection, once the designer has made a decision on their location.

These proposals from the computer are only available for his use if he so desires at this stage. This is still the earlier exploratory stage before a final hypothesis is established in DESIGN.

As the site details are known, it is now possible for the layout selected at this stage to be tested on the site. A visual display terminal output from the computer data base will show if desired all the details of the site with levels, and as the layout is manipulated upon this site, the effects of cut and fill, and similar criteria can be established once floor levels are decided. Because the activities and their positions are now decided, much of the furniture needs and equipment in *general terms* can be brought forward ready for use, providing of course, that the information base stores an adequate library.

If the Building Regulations and similar information are held in the Data Store, then clearly the proximity of the building to the boundary of another building, will bring forward any of the increasing needs as the distance is reduced, in the same way that the sound resistance of the partition was calculated. The solid-to-void ratio of elevations can be established, the effect of reduced window areas on lighting levels can also be examined, and the permissible volume within which the building has to be designed can also be determined by simple programs. There is a wide range of testing which can be carried out using the proposed Data Base before the design hypothesis is finally constructed. It is emphasized that this is still the pre-design stage, when alternatives are explored as a build up to the creative leap'. One of the characteristics of designers, is that they tend to come to very quick decisions about a design before all of the relevant facts are known, and reasonable avenues explored. Once a commitment is made, a defensive attitude is adopted, so that even the most severe criticism of a design will only serve to amend a design rather than start a new hypothesis. For this reason, it seems highly desirable that a final commitment is put off until all the preliminary examinations are complete. This should be to the designer's advantage, as well as the user's.

As an example, the water storage requirements of a building are often not established until long after a design has been conceived. Yet the storage tanks can be a very significant factor in the total design if for no other reason than structural load. Furthermore, it will probably be a professionally qualified man who will spend time seeking out this routine information. This, and much else like it, should be collected by input and stored in the Data Base ready for examination at the pre-design stage, and logged against checklists or other systems, to ensure that all data is collected.

It has become an unfortunate tradition, that the preparation of an estimate occurs after a sketch design has been prepared. Even multi-disciplinary team working seldom changes this approach, nor is the unsatisfactory nature of such a situation often questioned. At some stage, a design and a capital outlay have to be matched. More often than not, the amount of money which can be spent is known before work commences, or can be deduced from the needs. Cost limits can establish a budget, or a client may set the budget. The financial adviser, because of tradition and the inadequacy of his data, will invariably wait until the design is prepared before making a contribution, by which time, the architect has often committed himself to a chosen design, and will not be weaned from it. It is not the fault of individuals, but of tradition and training that makes the design team act in this way. The architect wants to be left alone on the one hand, and his specialist advisors are either not interested, or more usually, do not feel competent to assist in this pre-design stage. When cost planning does exist, this is usually derived from elemental cost breakdowns produced by a number of organizations. These have been of use, but apart from being limited, they are not always compatible with each other. Furthermore it is questionable whether these factors are the most satisfactory for cost analysis or cost planning. Clearly, many of the items such as ironmongery are of little cost importance before a design has been proposed. Many other categories in these cost analyses cannot reasonably be considered at such an early stage of the design. It is also less than satisfactory to think of costs in material terms rather than functional terms. It is clearly necessary to think of a roof, roof structure, and ceiling, as one item because it is together that they fulfil functions such as sound transmission, and therefore must be considered together in cost terms. To deal with each in isolation, and making savings on one and then another part of the whole function can lead to the deficiences in the total function so commonly seen.

The factors most likely to affect the cost of a project are:

1. Location
2. Area
3. Number of floors in which the area is contained
4. Type of envelope and its shape
5. Division of internal spaces
6. Type of construction
7. The intensity of servicing
8. Energy input requirements
9. The designer
10. The brief

This is not an exhaustive list by any means, but even in this short list, a substantial difference from the conventional analyses is shown.

The personality and inclinations of the individual designer is a very important factor in the cost of the building, as every quantity surveyor or contractor knows, but this doesn't show itself in conventional systems.

Energy input (8), can be automatically derived from the type of envelope and shape (4). Intensity of services (7), can be automatically deduced from the brief (10).

When one looks at a sketch plan, which is often used as the basis of a cost forecast even for very large contracts, one sees that this provides little more information than is included in this list. Certainly, many of the traditional cost analysis items cannot be deduced from these drawings, and yet an estimate is proposed.

An examination of the factors which would most likely interest a contractor at this stage gives yet another list, roughly as follows:

1. Availability of labour for the area
2. Location
3. Commencement and possible completion date of contract
4. Complexity
5. Size of project in
   (a) area
   (b) height
6. Site difficulties, e.g. location of stores, pumping etc.

He would probably not include materials, as he would assume that these would be measured and that he would be paid for them. He is really concerned with factors which affect the management of resources, rather than the resources themselves. Even though these lists may not be very comprehensive, it is strange that they all look so different. This is partly because a lot is 'read into' other pieces of information. Site difficulties can often be deduced from a location plan and local knowledge and so on. But the real reason is because at this stage, any system is highly speculative, and probably one set of choices is as good as another, as the human brain will compensate or load any of the parts to make the end result come out to what seems reasonable. If this seems an outrageous idea, how then does the architect, with little experience of detailed cost, and often without help or guidance prior to his design, produce a sketch plan within the right target area of a budget? Everyone gets the feel of the cost of a job, and this pervades any system. There is one thing which the system unfortunately cannot do, and that is to forecast what will be the market price at the time a tender is sought. Because traditional systems, in the main, preclude any other ways, we operate a system whereby the major speculation which can affect the price, i.e. the market conditions (irrespective of inflation) is unknown until all of the documentation has been carried out. In addition, in the early stages, we surprisingly use a tool which does not overtly include this speculation on the market conditions in its format.

Fine (1974) suggests:

'There are several alternative approaches to meeting tendering strategy requirements. An excellent workable strategy for many firms, for example, is to accept at random one or more of the alternative choices of contract available whenever the workload appears to be low. An alternative policy would be to be selective within the range of opportunities offered on a basis dependent upon attitudes held within the firm. One view could be to obtain work at any price because there is sufficient understanding of the legal and contractual processes to be able to read the fine print to the firm's advantage. And another alternative is that of attempting to understand the working of the economic sub-system in the construction industry and to use the knowledge gained. Of course a mixture of strategies is possible, and the understanding of one process need not inhibit the use of another . . .

Another view of estimating is obtained by looking at the whole task and breaking the task down into a set of sub-tasks in order to estimate the cost of each of these sub-tasks. The total cost estimate is then the sum of the cost estimates of each sub-task. This method of estimating is the one most frequently claimed as being used in the construction industry. The users believe the method to be precise and claim that, provided care is taken not to omit any sub-task, good results are always obtained.

Some organizations claim that Bills of Quantity form an analysis that provides a suitable basis for this method. Examination of BQ bids by various contractors leads to some doubts about this claim. The bills presented by various contractors in bidding for certain jobs have been examined. The bids were for work ranging from motorway, hospital and school construction to housing. There were no significant differences between the conclusions drawn from the different classes of work. The bills were examined item by item. Taking each of the five competitors in each contest, the value of the bidder's price divided by the mean price was calculated. The distribution of values obtained was then examined: the range of values was from 0 to 5 when the mean was unity and the standard deviation of the distribution was 0.45 times the mean. The significant items did not appear to be any more consistent than the insignificant ones. On one motorway contract there was a factor of 4 between the highest and the lowest rates for concrete paving, as presented by the contestants.'

This extraordinary situation could surely only prevail if there was no alternative method, and this will be examined later. In the meantime, we can consider possible aids at the pre-design stage even using this traditional approach.

The first factor which will affect the cost, is that of Regulations and other legal and administrative requirements for the type of project chosen. The definition of the number of children in a school automatically gives data, such as a minimum teaching area, number of sanitary units, and many other minimum requirements. In the case of offices, the Shops and Offices Act again defines minimum work spaces and requirements of sanitary units, and environmental criteria. Therefore, it is possible for Data Store, by simple mathematical processing, to give a minimum building brief requirement. To this must be added a number of items which are the personal choices of the Designer, or Design Team. These include:

1. The additional area to be given
2. The complexity of the design proposed
3. The construction

As all estimating is so speculative at this stage, the budget may just as well be created by taking an area/cost, and adding percentages for items 2 and 3 above plus a further percentage for the speculation of the tender situation. Once a target has been set, it will invariably be achieved by some means; either by scaling up to standard, or by reducing the standard of the building fabric. The major problem is to try to find a basis for wise spending: to establish whether the cost benefits are in favour of single storey building or multi-storey; whether complexity of plan form is justified: or whether area is more important than the quality of the building fabric.

The problem therefore gradually changes from one of how much can be built for the money, to one of what should be built and in what form. This may seem normal and obvious, but most buildings fall below reasonable functional standards, and this is usually blamed on shortage of money. In these cases, the client is seldom told that he is getting a sub-standard building, quite often because the effects of cost savings on performance are just not known. If these were known, the client might either choose to spend the extra money, or request a re-apportionment of the money. Maybe even the designer would have re-apportioned the money had he known the effects of his decision at an earlier stage. Before the energy crisis, building insulation was an early victim to cost savings, but the effects on running costs were rarely made clear to the client. It is often said that the client wouldn't pay the extra, but on what evidence was he asked to make this judgement, if any? There are innumerable examples which show that

(a) sub-standard building can be taken to be a norm, and
(b) that the apportionment of the budget is unbalanced.

59

In the latter case, the agreed budget can be apportioned in a whole variety of ways. Cheap roof, expensive walls. Expensive inside, cheap outside, or extravagant front and cheap rear as was common in the 1930's. There is no absolute rule, but there are two major ways of approaching the problem.

1. To apportion the money before the design starts in accordance, and in agreement with the client's needs. Does he want low maintenance costs, expensive image, large area, and so on.
2. To make an instinctive design, and develop the project until the budget runs out.

Most designers would deny doing the latter even if they couldn't agree to doing the former, but it is nevertheless true that it is still comparatively rare for the apportionment of cost to be considered according to priority of need, as opposed to tradition. For example, for many decades felt roofing was denigrated, but at the same time, selected for most jobs on the basis that there was no money for anything more expensive. But it would be absurd to say that the foundations could not be afforded, or the car manufacturer not to supply wheels because the budget would be exceeded. Clearly, the process must be one of establishing the requirements of the building enclosure in functional terms for the carrying out of the activities in the brief. When these criteria have been established, then a budget is proposed and apportioned so that the criteria can be met. If the figure exceeds the client's budget, then he, the client, must either find more money, or become party to the reduction in standards made wherever these might be, and also told of the implications of these reductions. In an increasing climate of claims against designers, it will be no excuse to say that there wasn't money available to do the job properly if this was not made clear to the client at the outset. Nor even to design shorter life buildings than the law would expect to be a norm, without first obtaining the client's written agreement. As we have seen, there is no optimum, no absolute, and so the client *must* be a party to the apportionment of the budget in any project, but this will mean making earlier design decisions for some items than is usual, and if the budget is to be at all realistic, the period between design and tender must be reduced to an absolute minimum. For as we have seen, the estimate itself is speculative, but when the forecast has also to include the further speculation of time, i.e. what the market will be like months ahead, the total variability can be enormous. This unforecastable market effect was seen in 1975, where labour and materials kept rising but tenders dropped because of a competitive market situation. No one could forecast the effect of this upon tenders months ahead. No cost advisor can reasonably expect to cope with this situation, and the client cannot be expected to go on with either finding more money, or having a sub-standard building. It is doubtful whether he will be prepared to continue to ignore the maintenance and cost in use implications which are incurred due to reductions made in the design standards, in order that the tender can be reduced. All of these issues raise the question of whether the actual design, synthesis, creative leap, or whatever one calls it, must be made in a more interactive fashion with the client user and the design team, resolving these aspects of the proposal together, and drawing

60

upon data store to give instant evaluation of each hypothesis until an agreed balance is made.

The methods described so far can help to make this improved user/designer interaction a possibility, and in addition, can be incorporated into a total system of design and construction information flow.

Chapter 4
DESIGN

Having identified the major components of the brief, produced and ordered the appropriate data, the designer can begin his design work, one of the principal aims of which is to provide a hypothesis, or a series of hypotheses for consideration by himself, the design team, and the client/user. But in order to set up some criteria by which these hypotheses will be judged, one is immediately faced with having to make some examination of what architectural design really means. Again, some fundamental re-thinking is obviously needed, even though this important subject can only be touched upon here.

One is immediately struck by some very odd discrepancies in our normal thinking about design. For example, it is strange that the early Greeks, whose architecture has probably achieved more general approval than any other, did not consider architecture as an art, but a craft. This classification is understandable because, except for a few rare occasions, the functional need for the building to satisfy simple physical needs must inevitably curtail the potential for free creative thought. Recently even this free creative thought has been increasingly related to possible deep structures of the mind with the limitations that these might impose, particularly as it is suggested that these are hereditary structures. Bernstein has related these deep structures to music. He suggests that Chomsky's deep structures, which operate through transpositional processes in the neural mechanism to a surface structure, which is our everyday language, relate to prose with the functional purpose of communication. But this is not poetry. Music on the other hand has no functional purpose of communication, and therefore does not relate to prose, but to poetry. Or in other words, not to a surface structure, but to a super-surface structure. It seems possible that in this lies a danger, not only of making direct comparisons between architecture and the work of Chomsky, but also of grouping architecture together as a single whole. If architecture is broken down into the three groups already proposed, the following relationship can be suggested.

Prestigious — Poetic
General — Prose
Conservation and — Poetic and Prose
Infill

That is not to say that only the prestigious should have care, or that the general should be mediocre. Far from it. The General category may well improve if the pressure of trying to achieve an artistic work is removed. Concern for space may take a higher importance. Georgian architecture is only one example where standard functional shells had only minor modifications to identify local or personal need.

It might also be relevant to question whether architecture should be analysed from the deep structures of language, rather than the symbolism of vision which has been part of living things long before there was speech. It might be that the deep structures of visual symbols are much deeper and influence the structure of language, and that it is the symbolism and language of vision which is the more important to architecture.

The value and necessity of research such as this cannot be questioned, but nevertheless it is worth bearing in mind that this may not help the creation of better building, or better language. There have been many analyses of buildings throughout history showing how different formulae and angles, such as the Golden Section, apply to certain beautiful buildings, but these do not appear to help to improve the standard of the poor designers as far as can be detected. It is wise to consider design analyses and methods from time to time on their potential for improving performance, rather than as an academic study. This must similarly apply to the proposals in this book.

Our lack of understanding about art and architecture, as well as the need to satisfy practical functional needs, particularly for the general category of building, must inevitably make the design task extremely difficult to say the least. In fact, this is probably the first time in history that the idea that every building should be a potential work of an artist has even been proposed. In the past, only a limited number of buildings had more than a pragmatic solution to a human need. An architect or designer, in the modern sense, was only rarely used for self-conscious design. Not only are these rare buildings referred to over and over again in any works of architecture, which raises the question of whether this constant imprinting of the mind of a limited number of buildings is very akin to brain-washing, but these special category buildings were always related to wealth, where deficiencies in functional performance could be paid for by using more labour and resources than were available to the common man. In other words, functional deficiencies could be counteracted by a waste of resources. This Renaissance approach has persisted into the twentieth century, and spread into a wide range of buildings where such waste cannot be afforded.

It is to be hoped that the prestigious architecture will always exist, but it would be as ridiculous to assume that all buildings should be in this category as it would be to assume that every car should be a handmade Lamborghini, or every piece of furniture should be designed by Makepeace. These prestigious buildings should explore the frontiers of thought and construction which will then, gradually, be absorbed into the general building category in the same way as it has done in the past.

It is interesting to consider that even these special buildings may begin to portray a new democratic thought process as suggested earlier. It is important to consider this suggested difference between prestigious architecture and general architecture because it will create a difference in emphasis in the use of the data bank, even though it will not be a difference in kind. Just as repetitive production of components reduces costs, the repetitive use of groups of data will be cheaper than individual searches for every project as might happen for special buildings. For example, the prestigious building will contain a great deal more cross searching of the files, similar to lateral thinking, and the general category will have a greater amount of predetermined sequential logical steps. Even if this categorization is accepted, it is still necessary to pursue the basis of architectural design a little deeper whilst at the same time trying to avoid a commentary on aesthetics, so that we may uncover a little about the processes and products for which information will be used. The designs which are rated most highly are, without exception, unique: but that is not to say that everything in the design is unique. Even in a building design such as St. Catherine's College, Oxford, where Jacobsen designed such items as furniture and cutlery, he did not design the locks, door closers, and many other parts of the building. It is therefore important to realize that however creative our input into building design may be there are many components within these buildings which are almost always 'taken from the shelf', or not designed from scratch. These include ironmongery, doors, light-fittings, ceiling finishes, roof lights and so on, and on. A very considerable number of buildings are designed from a pre-designed set of parts, and therefore the synthesis consists of putting together these pre-designed parts. This is rather like making sentences with pre-designed words, which we all do, and which we quite accept. Some buildings are designed with specially-designed components incorporated, but even where the content of these is high, there will most certainly still be a large standardization of those components within that building. Ceilings, for example, remain fairly constant except for special areas, and this also applies to doors, floor finishes, and so on. If there wasn't such a discipline of standardization, the building would be too confusing to the eye, and therefore unacceptable. This must lead us to the conclusion that there is a high level of predesigned components, or alternatively repetition in every building.

This idea is not to be confused at this stage with industrialized building, because there are two aspects of standard components, or the repetitive use of components.

1. The standardization of the idea of a component, because of the limitations of the craftsman's mind and the user's mind.
2. The standardization of the component for ease of manufacture and erection.

If we look at history to test the validity of this proposition, we see that standardization has been more normal than the opposite, for the reasons already given. The Romans used a standard idea throughout the empire which was then used for local manufacture.

Kurent (1971) has shown how ideas on modular sizes were transmitted:

> 'Modular sizes of Roman building components are small multiples of various standard units of sizes. Compositions of Roman building components are consequently sums and multiples of various standard units of sizes. A length of a building, for example, was chosen by a Roman Architect as a multiple of a Roman standard dimensional unit. It was easy to transform such a length into various sums and multiples of

smaller standard sizes and hence the building's articulation. Vitruvius emphasized this principle by telling architects to respect diligently the ratio of symmetries, i.e. the ratio of componible sizes.'

It must have been the same for details as it was for the modular dimensions which predisposed the shapes and positions of buildings, and even the layouts, of Roman towns. More recently, it has been the manufacture of components which has become more important as the basis of standardization and centralization.

If then we leave infill and conservation for the moment, and consider how this information can help the Prestigious and the General Categories, we can see:

1. That a large number of pre-designed units can be kept in a library based upon a dimensionally-coordinated system.
2. The prestigious building will make less use of this library, but as fashion leaders, they will probably become a source for providing new units to put into the library.

But whilst we may be able to accept a library of pre-designed units, we have no rules and no scale, and this may be at the heart of the problem.

When a musician writes notes on a musical score, those symbols indicate a very specific musical vibration, but when a designer uses fairly generally accepted symbols, these are not in the least bit specific. From the point of view of an information flow, this is the equivalent of giving a conductor a piece of music where the tonal values of the symbols are constantly changing, and then giving him a thesaurus, or some other documentation, for clarification. The design team at present invariably transmit their thoughts by the use of symbols on paper, and yet the contractor could have a multitude of interpretations for even a simple symbol like that for a manhole or wall, both of which are in common use.

Can there not be a rational set of symbols which will not inhibit the designer unreasonably? There have already been some steps in recent years which help us in this direction. One of these is the Dimensional Coordination papers produced by the Department of the Environment, and which have been significant in rationalizing the dimensioning of three-dimensional space.

Although the principles of dimensional coordination have been known and propagated for many years, it is a subject which is so important to this thesis that it is worth recapitulating on some aspects of its development.

Kurent (1971) has described how dimensional coordination was of considerable importance to the development of Roman architecture, and he makes clear how well developed their systems were in the following illustrations (Figures 25 and 26).

These dimensionally coordinated planning units, as applied to a building is shown below, and is extraordinarily reminiscent of a design for an industrialized building system.

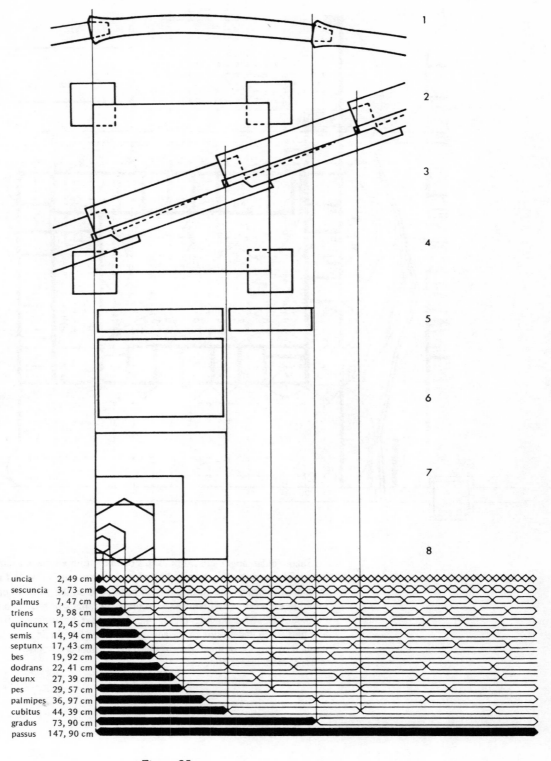

uncia   2, 49 cm
sescuncia   3, 73 cm
palmus   7, 47 cm
triens   9, 98 cm
quincunx   12, 45 cm
semis   14, 94 cm
septunx   17, 43 cm
bes   19, 92 cm
dodrans   22, 41 cm
deunx   27, 39 cm
pes   29, 57 cm
palmipes   36, 97 cm
cubitus   44, 39 cm
gradus   73, 90 cm
passus   147, 90 cm

Figure 25

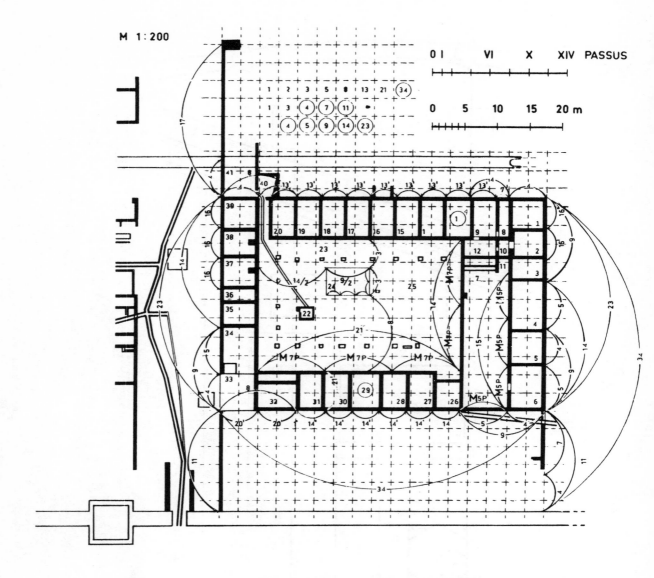

'The modular length and width of this building from Emona are multiples of 1 passus. The modular length and width of its atrium are multiples of 7 passus. The rhythm of rooms on the north side is 13 pedes, and on the south 14 pedes. Three rooms in the western and two rooms in the eastern flank of this building are in the rhythm of 16 pedes. Modules of 13, 14 and 16 pedes are deviations from the module of 3 passus (15 pedes), due to the adaptation of the type building to the size of insula (city block). In short, various multiples of standard Roman units of sizes were in use as modules for buildings'.

Figure 26

68

Kurent continues:

'A by-product of the fall of the Roman Empire was the loss of standard (human) sizes in a large part of the world. Gothic architecture had to substitute geometry and its irrational quantities for arithmetical rational modular methods. The Renaissance attributed to the module only its aesthetic role; there were too many various feet, cubits and inches in Europe to achieve the practical role of componible modules. Finally, the perfection of our numerals and decimal calculation has made our civilization unaware of the advantages of simple componible integers'.

We have strayed so far and for so long from the proper standards of dimensioning, that we tend to overreact to any standardization in case we lose our freedom. But can we, or even should we, resist that much? The *Architects' Journal* (1971) states:

'With traditional building techniques, the space-enclosing elements of the building were usually manufactured and assembled on site. This gave the designer great freedom in selecting dimensions and sizes for the building; e.g. structure and walls were made *in situ* either of formless materials such as concrete, or of small cheap components such as bricks; both can be assembled on site to virtually any specified dimensions without much trouble. Also secondary elements, such as doors or windows tended to be made to specified sizes on site by craftsmen on a one-off basis.

In addition to the dimensional freedom they allowed the designer, traditional building techniques did not place much emphasis on accuracy, because there was always a following trade to make good the deficiencies of the previous one. If the structural frame was inaccurate, the bricklayers constructing the infilling panels could easily pull in, or stretch out, the brick courses to suit and cut bricks where necessary. Irregularities in the brickwork could, in turn, be made good by the plasterer, and inaccuracies in the plastered surface could be disguised by scribing the timber trim to the plaster face. Also, with one-off fabrication, components could be made to the actual sizes of the openings as measured on site, so that small departures from the figured opening sizes shown on the drawings were of little importance.

However, with component building, the manufacturing and assembly processes are separated; the former being transferred from the rough and ready conditions prevailing on building sites to the controlled environment of the factory where labour can be employed more efficiently and higher manufacturing standards attained.

The use of large pre-finished components affects building design in two ways. First the problem of accuracy becomes extremely important; this is true regardless of whether the building method employed is industrialized or semi-traditional. If the component turns out to be oversized in relation to the opening left for it, it cannot be cut to size as bricks can be. On the other hand if it is undersized, problems of jointing will arise. And if the builder attempts to overcome these problems by setting up the component first and 'building

Controlling dimensions for housing

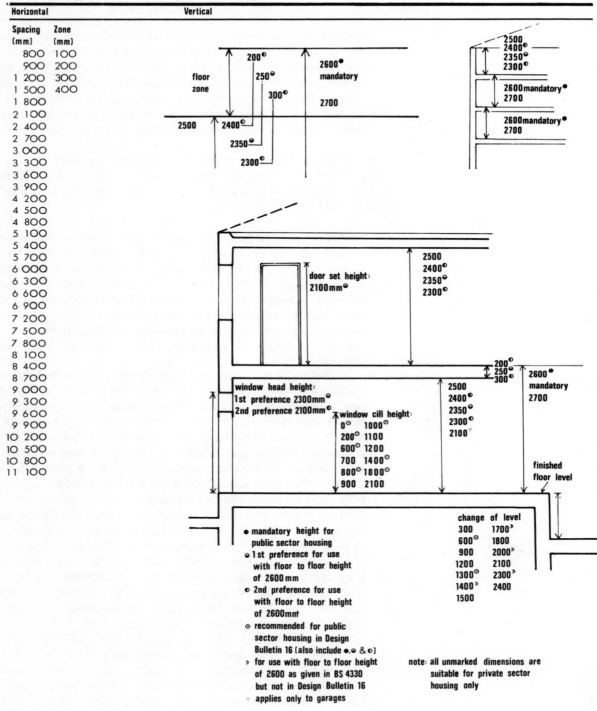

Horizontal		Vertical
Spacing	**Zone**	
(mm)	**(mm)**	
800	100	
900	200	
1 200	300	
1 500	400	
1 800		
2 100		
2 400		
2 700		
3 000		
3 300		
3 600		
3 900		
4 200		
4 500		
4 800		
5 100		
5 400		
5 700		
6 000		
6 300		
6 600		
6 900		
7 200		
7 500		
7 800		
8 100		
8 400		
8 700		
9 000		
9 300		
9 600		
9 900		
10 200		
10 500		
10 800		
11 100		

Figure 27

around it', instead of inserting it in a preformed opening, numerous problems arise: not only is early incorporation of prefinished components in the building carcass undesirable because of the likelihood of subsequent damage to them, but a rigid and possibly uneconomic operational sequence might be imposed on the building programme, and failure of the component to arrive at the right moment may delay everything else'.

A typical set of controlling dimensions for housing are shown opposite. Unfortunately, these controlling dimensions, even when accepted, are usually thought of individually as two-dimensional coordination on plan, and

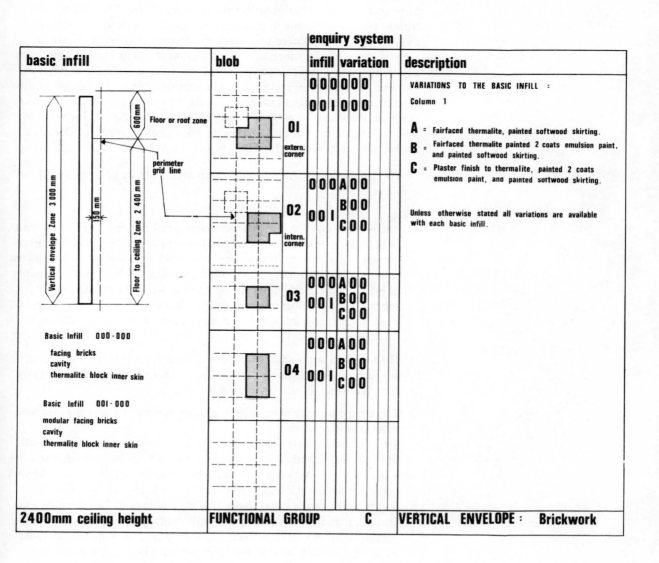

Figure 28

two-dimensional coordination in section, and for this one can probably blame the inhibitions of working on two-dimensional paper. But the potentials are there in the recommendations for three-dimensional rationalization of spaces. Length, width and height can be described in one graphic symbol if required. Therefore a library of walls, or partitions, or space dividers, can be constructed for all the rationalized height and width zones, and furthermore these can be recognizable to a computer. For example, a simple symbol with suffixes describing a cavity wall, could bring forward data which could be related to functional performance and contractual need, together with costs.

This simple description for the designer's use, can not only be interconnected by the data store with all necessary data for evaluation, but also be related to a further printout for the contractor's use. This will be dealt with in more detail in the next chapter but for the moment, it is sufficient to say that there is no need to provide the designer with more information than he needs for the selection of the component and its compatibility with adjacent components. This compatibility can be held within, and therefore known by the machine, by indicating its compatibility or non-compatibility with other components on the input sheets. This is simply the same techniques as those used in association charts for room usages and connections. This will enable the machine to indicate when two incompatible elements are being put together, and indicate this to the designer.

The important things in the construction of a library of blobs and symbols are:

1. The symbol with any suffixes must clearly indicate the scope of the unit or blob. (The word blob is used purely because it is a word which can represent a container of information, but which does not presuppose a component or unit quantity, or any other preconceived idea. It is a container of information of any desired shape, and which will be represented by a symbol). The essential point being that the rules for this blob or symbol must remain constant, whether these be rules for cost, construction, or whatever.

2. The blobs do not overlap each other. This is the problem with existing unit quantities and standard drawings, which are prepared almost at random, and with no rules to give a structure.

3. There must be a set of rules for each blob symbol. To take the manhole as an example:
   There is already a standard symbol for a manhole, but even if the depth of invert and materials were specified, it would not be clear what was the scope of the work to the team as a whole. How much, if any, of the pipes coming from the manhole is included? Is the excavation and backfill included in the symbol, and so on. If a set of blob rules for manholes were created, then the rules for the preparation of detail drawings, and the measurement of unit quantities, would be clear and all manholes would be compatible with the symbol. This symbol would also indicate size, and then only a suffix would be needed to indicate specification, which together, will indicate the designer's choice to the machine.

72

One of many ways of indicating to the machine which symbol and suffix are being used, would be to use a conventional drawing board to which are attached ultrasonic sensors along two edges as indicated below. This system will be used throughout this hypothesis because it is very compatible with normal processes, and therefore, most understandable to the majority of readers, and not because it is the only system, or necessarily the most suitable for all uses.

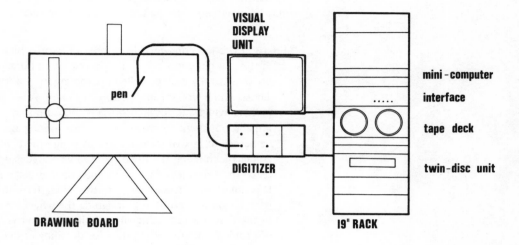

Figure 29

A special ball-point pen is used, connected by a wire to a control box, and which transmits an audio-signal as one draws. This signal is picked up by the ultra sonic sensors which can identify the position of the pen to within 0.25 mm. As the pen is moved around the board its position is monitored. If a set of symbols are fixed to the board either by means of a removable panel, or put on a pre-printed drawing sheet, the pen can be pointed at the symbol to indicate what one wishes to draw, and after that, the machine will record not only what, but where and how much. How much, in the case of line, and how many, in the case of units. This drawing equipment will of course need to be connected to a magnetic tape unit, or disk unit, for transmission to a computer bureau, or connected directly to a mini-computer. In this latter case, it is possible to also attach a visual display device which will enable the analyses and evaluations, previously described, to be observed and tested at the drawing board. The operation of such a system and the approach to equipment will be discussed in Chapter 9.

As the machine is able to recognize three dimensional space, it is able to retain information relating to that space. Therefore, as a design proceeds, the computer is able, for example, to build up on a grid basis the heat loss for every grid. Obviously those spaces nearer the external envelope will have larger losses than internal ones, and this will be seen. By calling up a menu of heat emitters, such as radiators, it is a simple matter to equate the output of the emitter to the loss. This means that the engineer and the architect can work together on their preliminary layout of engineering services.

Other more sophisticated programs are available, which record the effect of solar heat gain and shading on the building for any day and time of the year. The visual effect of this shading can, of course, be seen on the perspective which the program can bring forward.

As the whole process is developed, it will be seen that these blobs and symbols enable information, such as tender costs, and performance of the works, to be called up at any stage and given consideration.

Before going into further details about the machine and the process, it may be worth considering the implications so far:

Firstly, there is a considerable number of items which could be rationalized in the manner described, and inserted into a library for common use in order that they may be called up, merely by pointing a pen at a symbol. Those which would cause no anxiety at all would be manholes, roads, paths, pavings and foundations, etc. because they have little or no visual impact, but there are many more. Not so long ago it was considered to be heresy to talk of standard design components but increasingly design guides recommend the use of component shapes, and discussions even reach the extremes of the pro's and con's of pattern book architecture. It is not at all necessary to go to these lengths with this system but there is no longer any point in redesigning the wheel, or every window, and in any case it is becoming virtually impossible to do so, either because of problems of employing staff for detailing or because of the inability to keep up with the manufacturing processes.

Secondly, because there is such a large measure of standardization of component dimensions, brought about by dimensional coordination, every office or individual can create its, or his, own personal vocabulary of standard drawings which can also be added to the library.

Thirdly, all of the foregoing can also apply to the other professions structural, electrical, mechanical, landscaping, etc.

Fourthly, if this case is accepted, it can clearly be seen that up to, say, 80 per cent of any building could be designed using this standard library of symbols with an infinite range of suffixes for infills, some general, and some personal.

Fifthly, the remaining 20 per cent if such a proportion remains, can be dealt with by the preparation of new units from the basic materials and products file which is held in data store. This is in line with the present practice, where most of any building is fairly standard within itself, but where entrance halls, special rooms, etc., are treated differently.

None of these items impose any more restrictions on the designer than he imposes upon himself at present, the gains can now be considered:

1. Freedom from redrawing and respecifying repetitive items for the Architect and technician.
2. Freedom from remeasuring repetitive items for the Quantity Surveyor.
3. As the library can be double checked for accuracy, confidence in the standard of the details is built up by the whole team including the con-

tractor. (This may become the most critical factor when increases in building failure and legal actions are considered).

4. As the rules for each symbol have been rationalized, true comparison can be made between various infills as well as establishing the criteria for evaluation.

5. An opportunity to obtain instant evaluation of decisions, not only by the Architect, but by the whole design team.

Because the calculations for evaluation can be carried out, if desired, on an interactive basis, then the whole design team can work together to obtain the most suitable design hypothesis with the response time reduced to almost nil.

It is of course possible for the team, including the client/user, to sit before a variety of devices which give a visual output from the process, and to consider, as the design proceeds, the likely capital cost, cost in use under various headings, daylight and artificial lighting levels, solar shading and solar gain, and structural evaluation, right up to the production of the perspective. A perspective can be produced at any stage, and can be turned round, or the angle of view changed, or rotated, at will. Obviously, if only the main building shape has been input, the perspective will only be of this. As the design proceeds, more and more is shown. (See Appendix for illustration of this point.)

Whilst the system does not enforce team design any more than the present system does, it certainly offers great advantages to work this way. This may raise some of the old criticisms of team work in design, but even the most individual of people has to work as part of a team, no matter how much he may persuade himself that he doesn't. He usually does this by keeping his associates at a long distance, thereby increasing the length of response time.

Jones (1970) comments on Designing by Committee as follows

'Our distrust of committees of designers seems to owe something to myth-makers such as Northcote Parkinson (1958) and to such wise-cracks as 'a camel is a horse designed by a committee'. It is doubtful if this view fits the facts: there are plenty of complicated things, such as automobiles, hospitals and missile systems for which major design decisions have been successfully taken by committee and could not have been taken by one person. Perhaps we have not learnt to distinguish between the ineffectual majority of committees, in which the chairman and the members are unskilled at collaborative decision making, and the minority of highly influential committees in which the chairman and members have been selected for the relevance of their knowledge, for their understanding of each other's spheres of interest and for their ability to collaborate. Committees of the second kind are particularly to be found within large international corporations, technical agencies and military planning groups in which everyone is committed to a common interest which makes him an 'organization man'. We may disagree with the narrowness of these interests but we should admit that, within them, it is possible to make effective design decisions by committee'.

Whilst on the one hand, one brain cannot hold all of the information necessary for all of the complete design decisions of a building, the methods of group working have not yet been perfected, but where they have been used successfully, the outcome has been outstanding. A team which can now include the client and/or user, will be able to use symbols like words to improve our conversation. These symbols, or blobs, can be used at any appropriate level. At the lowest level, individual doors and ironmongery can make up a door set; this door set can become a higher level unit to be incorporated into an even higher level unit until one has, for example, a whole house.

These higher level blobs can be used to make designs for more houses, or the whole house can be used as a standard blob if desired, and therefore standard houses can be put together to form an estate in the same way as at present. Although these blobs can be as small as one wishes, for economy, the scale of the blob should be the largest reusable item. The definition of the blob and its rules is a decision of the users, with the proviso that it is a unit of description and measure which is ot common value to the whole design and construction team, and not just an arbitrary symbol for the Architect's benefit. Quantities are therefore capable of being premeasured as well as all the other characteristics of the blob, not only in functional criteria, but as a basis for construction management. These blobs can take a wide variety of forms

1. The manhole type, previously described, which defines a cohesive unit.
2. The space divider type, which defines a three-dimensional space into which infills are placed.
3. The defined type blob. This might be the plumbing content in a house or a whole bathroom blob which could contain all the parts of a bathroom to a given standard, and which the designer is able to manipulate as he wishes.

Obviously, the more people that group together to make a library, the quicker it will grow, and therefore the greater will be the choice and the more economical it will be for keeping it updated.

It may be asked what advantage this has over traditional standard drawings and unit quantities.

Standard drawings have an inbuilt prejudice against them because they are rarely structured for ease of retrieval, and usually prepared and selected comparatively at random. Unit quantities can only be selected by the Quantity Surveyor by guessing which items may be expected to be repeated by the designer, and this invariably means that they have to be modified.

Even when there is goodwill to overcome these difficulties, there remains a major disadvantage. Because the item to be standardized has not been select in accordance with a predefined plan, there is almost certain to be an overlap with adjacent items which will cause the designer to think that whilst he is making alterations and amendments, he may as well redesign the item. Tank rooms are a common target for standard drawings, but they are rarely drawn to cope with variations in size, but worse, they will usually show a roof structure which will, most likely, not be required for succeeding jobs. Within a rationalized set of blob rules, the tank room would have been a contained item, showing only its relationship to the roof structure, and not the roofing and the structure itself. This would be in another part of the library with an indicator as to its compatibility. Because of the preciseness of the blob, the quantities can be taken off and stored with confidence. Furthermore, because the designer will quickly remember the details of these standard assembly drawings, he will only need a catalogue showing him the symbol for the item and the possible infills that are in the library. This is the same as the look up for a catalogue of sanitary fittings or similar items, where only the minimum for the designer's needs are shown. There is a secondary advantage in that it is tempting for the designer to make minor and unnecessary modifications to the standard drawings, purely because of his creative nature, which can in turn cause havoc for the Quantity Surveyor and the remainder of the team if they have used these as a standard for their work. In the case of the cataloque, this is more likely to be accepted as it stands, particularly when time has shown the high quality and reliability of the details.

When we apply the system to a computer there is an even greater advantage. In the traditional system, one commences a design with the whole confusing world of data before one. In the computer system so far described, a lot of irrelevant data has been eliminated from the project file by the choice of site and brief. But there is still a fairly formidable quantity of possible data on materials and components to be faced, if a true analysis is to be made. If the catalogue in the computer is appropriately labelled, the naming of the type of project itself will remove many items which are not applicable from the selection area. There is no point in sorting through the sanitary fittings for a primary school if one is designing an Old People's Home. Similarly, once the heights of the various parts of the building have been established, there is no point in the computer offering items which are not compatible with these heights. It can therefore be seen that each project creates its own data selection area, rather than working to the conventional pre-defined hierarchies, and many of the selection areas can be reduced by the computer as decisions are made.

There is of course, nothing to stop one overriding these pre-selectors if it is desired, but normally, these time saving advantages will be used. The insertion of a window on a plan will automatically be shown on the elevation, and *vice versa*. This same approach is applicable to a wide range of items which is not only time saving, but acts as a cross check.

The running cost of appropriate computing equipment for such a system is difficult to define as it is often rented, partly because of the favourable rental terms when considered in the present tax environment, and partly because new models are announced fairly frequently. Therefore the capital cost of any item, divided by five, might be a reasonable basis for calculating hiring cost. If this is assumed, the hired cost per annum of the ultrasonic unit and pen, together with control box and magnetic tape drive unit might be approximately one fifth of one average technician's salary (including overheads) per annum. To supplement this with a mini-computer with visual display for interactive use would cost approximately one technician's salary on the same basis. Therefore a total inhouse system, with facilities for linking with a large central computer unit if desired, would give a hired cost of approximately the equivalent of less than one-and-a-half technician's salary per annum. A technician's salary has been used as a unit of measure and not for any other implied reason. If one wishes to use a little initiative, the whole of that described can be obtained for the price of a medium priced car. This comparatively small capital cost would enable the collection of much of the data for a small building system for processing by a bureau. The question must then arise as to what benefits we can derive at this stage, let alone any of those yet to come.

The client, user, and any member of the design team are able, subject to the data store being adequate, to sit around this equipment, elucidate the brief and manipulate this into a bubble diagram form; relate this to its site and environment, and mould these bubble diagrams into a building form with appropriate performance criteria from which materials and components can be selected. The building hypothesis can be proposed as an integrated whole, and tested not only against Building Regulations, but for most other environmental criteria. Within hours rather than days, weeks, or months, the client user is able to know how much his building will cost to build, to maintain, and to run, and the performance of the building in general. In addition, he is able to see what it would look like both from the outside and the inside. Depending upon the equipment used, it is also possible to have a visual interpretation of what it is like to walk in and around the building. These are the gains which are obvious — speed, reliability of better quality data, immediate evaluations, and visual understanding for the client user as part of a team. But it is important to consider possible losses. The losses can be described as follows:

1. Changes from a conventional way of working, involving possible retraining. There is very little retraining as such, it is more a question of changing attitudes. With regard to work changes and the possible problems that this might bring, there are undoubtedly some to be resolved. For example, the work is more concentrated, decisions have to be made more quickly, and this means that changes in working arrangements are sometimes necessary and these will be discussed, but it is interesting to hear the views of a trade union leader, Cooley (1971), in a booklet issued by the Technical and Supervisory section of the Associated Union of Engineering Workers.

'One is frequently asked if technological change is a good thing or not. This is really a non-question. It depends entirely how it is used and who controls it. We need not have any fear of technological change. It is in fact merely an extension of man's own capabilities. Historically man sought to extend his eyes by using telescopes, ranging from the time of Galileo to today where he uses radar and radio telescopes. He extended his tongue and his ears by communication systems and audio aids. His muscular power he extended through mechanization, and his energy he extended and increased through the harnessing of nuclear power. Even the most sensitive faculty of man, that of memory and his nervous system, he has now in many ways extended by the decision making techniques used through computers. It was us and people like us who used their great skill and ingenuity to create all this technological change.

Our members long to be able to use that skill and ingenuity to provide the material basis for a more full and dignified existence for the community as a whole. This drive for further scientific knowledge "into that untravelled land whose margin fades forever and forever when I move" is to be welcomed; indeed it is one of the guarantees of our future prosperity. It must not however be a blind unthinking drive forward. As the main Union whose members design much of the equipment described in this booklet we have a social and political responsibility to analyse its effects upon our members and the class to which they belong in our profit-orientated society'.

2. The variety of design will be restricted by the size of the library. This is of course true of the human creative act as well, but in the long run the computer library, by using selective sortation, could offer a choice from a far greater bank of knowledge than the human brain could encompass, or that which he would normally find possible to handle in traditional form. It is also worth considering a designer's method of working in relation to this point. As we have seen, it is almost inconceivable for a designer to design everything from scratch in each new design and that only a portion is newly created. Therefore the designer's mental library proceeds rather like the motion of a caterpillar.

Figure 30

The information gained on the last project is digested, and those parts which were successful are incorporated into the next job, and a limited area, probably the least successful parts of the last project are reconsidered. This may then form the base for the next move forward.

3. Team design. This is a criticism which may be made by some, and has been previously discussed, but the general pressure of society is moving the traditional methods of design into this form of working. In any case, the process can be used individually and slowed down to the pace of the traditional method if desired. The pace is a personal choice, as with all other aspects of the system.

4. The major criticism is that the gains in time will be frustrated by the administrative procedures for planning, etc. This criticism will be dealt with more fully later, but it may be noted here, that most of the machinery which inhibits the process has been put there to safeguard against the deficiencies of the present system of designing one-off buildings without any means of evaluating them, either in themselves, or against the background of the environment. Maybe it would be possible to take back into the design team's responsibility some of those things which it has foregone if the situation is changed by using these strict evaluative techniques.

79

Having discussed some of the possible disadvantages, we might return to the facility for visual presentation of moving in and around a building. It is a matter of interest to consider whether architecture would have taken a completely different form but for the invention of two-dimensional draughtmanship, probably developed from drawing in the sand or on papyrus. The reason for questioning this is that now, as never before, there are opportunities for designing in three dimensions. If is often claimed by architects that they design in three dimensions in their minds and that drawing in two dimensions is not inhibiting. This is patently not always true: there are failures at every level by designing in this way. Most water penetration problems occur at junctions which are almost impossible to draw in two dimensions. (Engineers use isometrics and axonometrics much more sensibly in these conditions.)

At the next level, the junctions of blocks and buildings are very often the weak points in the design because they are not readily evaluated in conventional drawing systems, and furthermore, the total environment for which the architect is often blamed is difficult to evaluate in two-dimensional presentations. Recent arguments on perspectives for important London buildings have highlighted this problem.

Next, the drawing board, tee square and set square have created a square world. It may be argued that buildings are rectangular because rectangular components are cheaper than curved ones; but obviously, each creates a demand for the other, and each emanates from the use of the tee square.

At the next level, one can see the terrible effects of two-dimensional designing in planning layouts, particularly in the case of estates, new towns, and cities. A visitor from outer space would never have believed that we don't have motor cars that turn at right angles when looking at some new town and city plans which are all too often based on the tee square and outmoded Renaissance concepts. Similarly, lines which may have been neat and sensible on a drawing, very often look absurd when traversing undulating ground in their final position. Buildings which have been set up with a tee square parallel to something convenient like a road centre line, often look incongruous because the real building is not read in conjunction with the original starting point for the tee square. But if we develop the data bank in the way described, and we build up our way of thinking in this multi-faceted way, it will be possible to design in three dimensions because the equipment is already capable of being used in this way.

In the meantime, there would be a great advantage in using models for creative design which can then be translated into the machine for evaluation. Models are usually made with extreme precision after the design is complete for the purpose of impressing the client or planning committee, but this is not only poor value in comparison with the working model, but usually they deceive client and designer, more than they clarify. Not only is there the potential for the design team to properly integrate their own facilities into a cohesive whole when using a creative design model, but the user is also able to make a proper contribution, which he finds almost impossible in the conventional drawing system. This is often a cause for his dissatisfaction with the built design. There is also the value of the working model on site, where site operators can actually visualize what they are doing and how their part relates to the whole.

This feeling for the three-dimensional will also, it is hoped, reflect itself in our evaluations. Up until quite recently, ideas were seen in terms of black and white, and this was reflected in ideas starting from God and the Devil and so on. We now see this to be not true. Yet, most analyses are evaluated on two-dimensional planes which promotes a yes/no or black and white type of evaluation. This in turn is further aggravated by hierarchic thinking. If one takes one simple example in building — energy conservation — what is the two-dimensional optimum for a given building volume?

1. Reduce surface area to minimum, i.e. sphere. But because of structural problems accept cube which causes lighting load and cooling load to increase.
2. Increase window area to reduce lighting load; now heat loss increases and solar gain increases.
3. Produce optimum shape for minimum artificial lighting; heat load increases.

Each change raises the question: How is the energy consumption for manufacturing materials used in the above solution affected? What is happening to the capital cost? What is happening to cost in use? How will it function?

It is quite clear that for every one subject area there are several interacting factors, and this does not even take into account the interaction of these items with other significant factors. These too are invariably considered, if at all, on the basis of two dimensional graphs which can clearly be misleading. One can now foresee the possibility of the visual representation of three-dimensional multiple matrices which will give a new feeling to the optimization of building design. There may be some that would argue that such refinements are quite unnecessary, just as it was argued that proper daylight evaluation was unnecessary as doing it by eye was good enough. How wrong this has proved to be. A look at the work already carried out over many years on farm building environments is chastening, because it shows that we take a great deal more care over the evaluation of an animal's physical environment than we do for man. Many people today are working in new buildings where these buildings are barely able to satisfy even the crude criteria laid down by law. Similarly, the spaces around buildings have been allowed to develop into wind tunnels, when there are already evaluative programmes which will assist in the forecast of troubles before they occur.

Public opinion and trade union pressures are likely to demand an increased standard, not only in design, but in performance and maintenance. In 1971 the *Architects' Journal* made this statement in their Handbook-Building Enclosure, and this is even more true today.

'There are signs that users' and clients' dissatisfaction with the poor performance of many modern buildings will become gradually too vocal to be ignored. In the past, architects have been liable to litigation usually only if a building suffered some specific failure or breakdown in fabric or services, or caused physical injury to a user. However, in a recent American case an Architect was taken to court for designing a school which severely overheated in summer — i.e. for failure of *overall* environment performance — and the client was awarded substantial damages.

As this trend grows (and it is certain to following the recent revision of CP3 chapter 11, and in the present climate of increasing consumer militancy), architects will have to overhaul their present haphazard procedures, think in a more disciplined way about the functions of the building fabric and the services it incorporates, and ensure that every decision taken — both by themselves and by the growing body of consultants, specialist manufacturers and subcontractors whom they direct — is compatible with the desired (and explicitly formulated) end result.'

An alternative argument is that of the return to simpler ways and methods which has already been partly argued. But the one consistent factor throughout mankind has been the trend towards more comfort, and less arduous labours. This has never changed and is not likely to change, so there will certainly be a demand for an ever increasing comfort level of building, built with a reducing labour force, and designed with reduced drudgery.

For all of these various reasons it is certain that a variety of computer aided design systems will be evolved for general use, but if the whole design team don't take sufficient interest at these early stages, they could find a rigid and unsympathetic system forced upon the industry. It is very easy to create a system which assumes standard rooms, parts of buildings, or even whole buildings.

It is also possible to largely dispense with the traditional design team in the presently accepted sense, and this could only be to the detriment of society. For we all want to create our own ideal world; and the computer specialists are no exception. It is very easy to become convinced that one has the perfect answer to all building, and to design a computer system to handle it, but there are some very real dangers which can emerge.

The first is the fact that the initial dedication and enthusiasm of the creator will not be maintained by the maintaining team which follows. A vast library of data can be quickly put together by enthusiasts; but who will maintain and update this great library? Therefore it is important for the system to be as self generating as possible. The second is, that those proposing the system may have a high intellectual ability and knowledge, but those that will be operating the system may not have the same capacity or dedication. The third, is that the computer system must not assume a building system even though one may be put into it. (The system operated at one time by the County Architect's department of the West Sussex County Council and described in the appendixes, was an open system, capable of accepting system building or traditional building, even though for quite a long time it mainly held a library of SCOLA components for architectural reasons.) If the system is not kept completely open, future generations may be chained to the system as no one will dare to tamper with such a complex situation, particularly if the originators have left. The computer must, as far as possible, only be considered to be the tool of the designer and not his master, and this tool he will certainly need.

Even when a fully operative sophisticated system is in operation, it is to be hoped that there will always be a proportion of design work which cannot be selected directly from the library, and so it is worth considering how this work should be evaluated from Communication to the Contractor.

It is often argued that the designer should become closer to the manufacturing and building trades in the industry, and there is a great deal of sense in this. But unfortunately, just as with the rest of the data problems, the tide is running too fast, and Architects, unable to cope, adopt different levels of consideration for different items. Metal items are dealt with much more superficially than joinery for example, where the Architect feels more competent to detail his needs very precisely. But even here, how close does he get to the true situation? If one takes this as an example, the Architect will detail his joinery requirements, but the chances that they will be made that way are quite remote. It may look as he expected, but the actual manufacture, jointing and so on, will be different because all the time, new tools and processes are being developed of which he is quite unaware. If he tries to correct this by making a study of these changes, he will be slipping behind on new techniques in other parts of the industry. It is certain that he can never keep abreast whilst change continues at the present rate. But there is something he can do. He can describe the appearance and performance of the article he desires, and this can be developed by the communication team working with the manufacturer to produce the answer he requires in the most economical way, thereby avoiding much of the waste caused by the manufacturer, either being held back by the delay in the designer's knowledge being brought up to date, or by converting the designer's drawings to a practical economic solution.

This is not a radical change. It happens all the time in large areas of the design communication process, and so it is only a question of rationalizing the process.

It would be in contradiction to the basic premise of this book to suggest that all that has been proposed in this chapter is a perfect answer to the problems of design. There are deficiencies in this proposal, just as there are deficiencies in the present system, or any other system. The real problem is to decide what society as a whole will demand, and make sure that whichever system is adopted, that it will be the best for client, user, designer and contractor, and if that future involves a computer system, the more that the design team becomes aware of the problem and works together, the better are the chances that a fair and workable system might emerge, giving increased participation with a faster response time.

Chapter 5

COMMUNICATION: DESIGN AND COST

The process of communicating the designer's intentions and obtaining a financial agreement has changed considerably over the last 150 years, and these changes have been well documented. Nevertheless, it is important to re-evaluate some of the problems.

Bills of Quantities and the present role of the Quantity Surveyor are little more than a hundred years old, and yet they have become such a norm in the United Kingdom that alternatives are perhaps too seldom considered. A proposal such as Design and Construct tendering is looked upon as a new idea, when most of its aspects used to be the norm. For centuries it was normal for the designer, master mason, or architect, to communicate his intentions directly to those craftsmen who would carry out the work. The reasons for the change are well known, but as with everything else so far, a return to fundamentals may be worth considering.

The problem of the communication of the design to the contractor falls into two parts

1. The transmission of the idea in the designer's mind to the mind of the constructor, if it is not the same person.
2. The establishment of a cost — both initial cost of design and any variations.

Both of these aspects have become bedevilled by the need to establish the fact that the most competitive cost has been obtained. Seldom is the most efficient or the fastest contractor sought, but almost always the one who can give the cheapest overall price. Theoretically, the prices that are given for each of the individual parts which make up this overall figure are a fair basis for pricing any variation. The fact that the contractor can and does manipulate and distort the individual prices within the overall sum is never questioned. This of course largely invalidates the competitive aspect once any variation is made. The criticisms of the existing system are well known to everyone, and therefore there is no point in going over this old ground and certainly not worth considering mechanizing such a system. If we look at the aspect of financial control first, it might be possible to establish some fundamental points as a base line.

What are the basic factors in creating a price, whether this be a Do It Yourself project, or a mammoth construction project?

(1)   The Cost of the Man

x

(2)   Activity time of the Man

+

(3)   The Cost of the Materials

+

(4)   The Cost of Plant

+

(5)   Profit (including Management)

These basic characteristics will be referred to by the following abbreviations.

Manpower	Mp
Activity	A
Material	M
Plant	Pl
Profit	Pr

These are very recognizable in the small project and in fact many additions and alterations are priced in exactly this way, but they become so obscure in the large contract that they can even be denied to exist. If we examine each of these characteristics in turn, we find that the cost of construction manpower is agreed nationally according to trades, and that this is a wage for time employed for the specific work done. The cost of the work is related to the time that the activity of carrying out the work takes. The materials are an obvious straight cost of purchase, and where Plant or equipment is needed, this is an additional cost to be spread over the activities to which it relates, quite often as a hiring charge. (There are some more complex aspects of plant which will be dealt with later).

Leaving aside Profit for the moment, one can see that the cost of, say, a wall would be:

The bricklayers cost per hour x the number of activity hours + cost of bricks and mortar + cost of plant

It may be that the cost of a bricklayer's mate should also be included, but that only follows the same pattern.

Each of the items, such as the bricks and the mortar, equally have to be made and these again follow exactly the same pattern which looks like Figure 31 opposite.

Gradually MpAMPl is added to MpAMPl until the whole structure is completed. This simple breakdown overcomes one of the major problems of coding systems already mentioned. Where does any hierarchical coding structure finish, the timber window? the window manufacturer? the timber supplier? the shipper? the forester? In hierarchical systems one can be easily drawn into eventually coding the world's products. But in this system the product of any level has criteria, and it is these criteria which provide

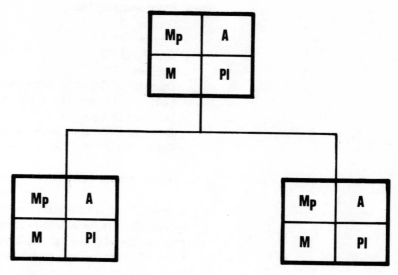

Figure 31

the code to be recognized. As it moves up the chain its criteria are changed, and therefore it holds a different place in the file and a new criteria code, and does not create a hierarchy.

Now we must consider the question of profit(Pr). Over and above the basic MpAMPl cost, there are the additional costs of management and profit. Management is included with profit, because whilst Manpower rates may be the same, the activity times the same (because very often it is the same manpower in use by different contractors) and also costs of materials and plants may be similar, there may be a difference in cost between two or more organizations. This occurs because of the level of management and the level of profit. Management in this situation refers to its efficiency in getting the best productivity from MpAMPl and its own cost, and for present purposes management and profit will be combined. One could therefore envisage the pricing of any project as being the amount of MpAMPl involved plus the Profit required to cover profit and management. Before profit and management needs can be examined, MpAMPl must be more closely defined and this we can do as though they were computer files.

Manpower. This would be a list of known and accepted building trades for which a short list of tradesmen, mates, and others might be as follows —

Bricklayer	Apprentice Electrician
Asphalter	Electrician
Roof Tiler	Fitter/Welder
Roofer	Bar Bender
Carpenter	Scaffolder
Joiner	Site Agent
Steel Erector	Foreman
Metalworker	Plumber
Fitter	Plasterer
Fitters Mate	Floor Layer

Floor and Wall Tiler
Glazier
Painter
Drainlayer
Labourer
Operator of Concrete Mixer, Pump or Compressor
Operator of Crane, Hoist, Elevators, Winch or Fork-lift Truck
Driver of Dumper
Driver of Excavator, Shovel, Bulldozer or Calf-Dozer
Driver of Vehicle, Tractor or Mechanical Barrow

There would be no more than say 50 types.

Activity. There is no precise time for an activity any more than there can be a precise rate for a building item, but there can be established reasonable and accepted average activity times which will provide a base line. These of course can vary in different parts of the country. Strangely, in an industry where there is probably more basic data than in any other industry, there is so little information available on such an important matter. True that Organization and Research, and Organization and Methods departments of large construction firms have these figures, and also that they are used for bonusing, but they are virtually unknown to the rest of the industry. This is incredible in itself, considering that this is the basic ingredient of cost and efficiency, but it becomes more incredible to appreciate the fact that little of this information reaches the estimator who uses a different set of criteria for estimating.

In the first instance we may assume that there will be about 500 activities. (Proposals for reducing this number will be described later).

Materials. This is obviously an endless list because new materials are being developed continuously, but for normal practical purposes, the list might contain say 3000 items.

Plant. This list is very dependent upon the type of Contractor and the type of work carried out, but will probably be in the order of 100 items.

Further, if one assumes that the general activities in the industry can be listed in unit terms as Figure 32, with the MpAMPI characteristics which are contained in the items set against them, we would have the basis for an updatable fundamental system.

But before proceeding further, we must question some of the basic statements to ensure that they are valid.

Can these files be prepared?
Can the files be updated?

It is curious and fortunate that most of the data that is proposed in the MpAMPI files is held at present by each contractor, to a greater or lesser extent, but it has little outlet in the present system.

FLETTONS IN GAUGED MORTAR (1:1:6)

	Mp	A	M	Pl

Half brick in wall, skin of hollow wall, dwarf wall or isolated pier (S.M.M. Cl. G3 (a) i, iii, iv, v).

Extra for curved work on half brick wall not exceeding 3 metres radius (S.M.M. Cl. G1 (d)).

Extra for curved work on half brick wall exceeding 3 metres radius (S.M.M. Cl. G1 (d)).

Extra over-gauged mortar for cement mortar (1:3) in half brick wall (S.M.M. Cl. G2 (b) iii).

One brick in wall, skin of hollow wall or dwarf wall (S. M. M. Cl. G3 (a) i, iii, iv).

One brick in isolated pier or chimney stack (S. M. M. Cl. G3 (a) v).

Extra for curved work on one brick wall not exceeding 3 metres radius (S. M. M. Cl. G1 (d)).

Extra for curved work on one brick wall exceeding 3 metres radius (S. M. M. Cl. G1 (d)).

Extra over-gauged mortar for cement mortar (1:3) on one brick wall (S. M. M. Cl. G2 (b) iii).

One and half brick wall, skin of hollow wall or dwarf wall (S. M. M. Cl. G3 (a) i, iii iv).

Figure 32

(a) Wage rates for various types of Manpower have to be kept
(b) Activity times are kept for bonusing purposes
(c) Materials costs are kept as estimates and invoices
(d) Internal plant records are kept for cost allocation, and external plant figures are supplied as hire charges.

Furthermore, if we examine the Schedules of Rates produced by the Department of the Environment, it is obvious that unit items can be prepared for all building work because they have already prepared them for the following ranges of building works.

Schedule 1   Schedule of Rates for Building Works
2   Schedule of Rates for Decoration Works
3   Schedule of Rates for Preparation-maintenance of Land
4   Schedule of Rates for Minor Works and Maintenance of Roads and Pavings
5   Schedule of Rates for Electrical Installations
6   Schedule of Rates for Electrical Distribution systems external to buildings
7   Schedule of Rates for Heating, Hot water and Ventilating systems

If these rates are broken down into their constituents of MpXA+M+Pl, and each of these basic files are updated as they can easily be, then the whole rate can be price updated at any time, provided that the rules are known. It is obviously impossible for all of the files to be correct to any one minute or hour, just as the published currency exchange rates are only as accurate as the communication system allows. But assuming a monthly update, as new wage rates are negotiated, the Manpower file will be updated and the computer can search through all of the items where the appropriate manpower type is used, and then update that item. Similarly for Materials and Plant, as new prices become available. Of course it is known that Contractors pay wages above the national scale and buy materials at special discounts, but this is immaterial to the present proposal because they will make allowance for these in their added percentage for management and profit. Good management will get good discount on goods and pay bonus rates where this is effective, and thereby keep the additional percentage down. That is the reward for good management. Activity times will only be refined where necessary and should not alter very rapidly or very often.

At this stage, we have a system which looks as follows in Figure 33.

These files can be established within an office, regionally, or nationally, but however or wherever they are set up, they can constitute the basic platform for payment for work.

If then the design team, on behalf of the client, invites contractors to give their percentage to cover profit and management and any other item they wish to include and which is not in the schedule, the computer could immediately produce a tender set of rates based on the percentage of the chosen Contractor.

Furthermore, if the blob quantities of the symbols are made up from this schedule, then it can be seen immediately that as the drawing is being produced, the tender can be known.

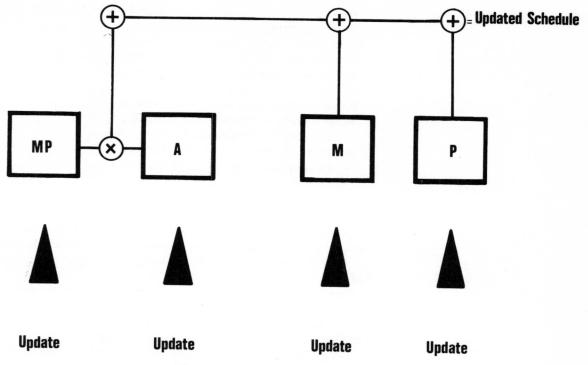

Figure 33

There are many additions and sophistications which can be made to the system. The Activities file is at present shown in a conventional form, but it is possible to restructure this file and then it becomes the same as the activity file we started with for the brief.

For example, the traditional Bill of Quantities may describe an item as follows —

Take from store and refix hardwood door and frame previously set aside for reuse . . .

The materials or item to be carried, is of no importance to the activity of the man. The man is concerned with how heavy, or how big the load is. If it is too heavy, he will need help, and if it is light but cumbersome, he will need help. This will affect the resources and therefore the cost. What is being carried is of importance in the materials file, but not in the activity file.

A very simple activity file can therefore be developed along the following lines.

Walking	Carrying
Climbing stairs	Stacking
Climbing ladders	Digging
Driving	Loading
Wheeling	Throwing
Lifting	Strutting

Hacking	Light hammering
Heavy hammering	Sawing
Positioning	Planing
Cleaning	Nailing
Placing Bulk Materials	Screwing
Placing Plastic Materials	Cutting
Spreading Plastic Materials	Threading
Working Plastic Materials	Bending
Spreading and finishing liquids	Connecting
Placing membranes	Erecting
Placing individual items	Dismantling
Fitting	

Another possible use of the activity files is to register the position of the site stores on the computer at an early stage, so that activity times of carrying from stores, etc., can be calculated automatically, an item surprisingly not covered in traditional systems but which is very significant to operation and cost.

Investigation of these items in depth could dramatically simplify the whole descriptive process, because again, we come to the point where the Bills of Quantities, by trying to bring together a pricing document and a descriptive document have complicated the process.

As the traditional system will naturally be defended, it would be sensible to assess the merits and demerits of the normal systems, sometimes, but not always, based on a Bill of Quantities; and the new proposals.

The demerits of the present system

1. The Bill of Quantities and similar systems take considerable resources to produce, in terms of measurement, calculation and printing. All of these processes are gone through for each contract, and priced by estimators for each Contractor invited to tender. This again is a considerable outlay in resource, for only one tender is accepted. The system is based upon the certain knowledge that large quantities of resources will be wasted. Costs of more than 5 per cent can be attributed to abortive tendering which are then added to costs of building. This abortive cost is of course included in every successful tender; and yet, it was to save costs and resources that the system was originally invented, albeit a different situation.

2. The Contractor is always in the position of quoting for projects, without knowing the reaction to any previous tender or tenders under consideration because of the very slow response time in the system. As his judgement on future tenders can only be based upon past performance of both jobs under construction and tenders submitted, he is always in difficulty. Fine (1974) observes:

> 'An analysis . . . . indicated that over a large part of the industry bids vary by about ± 10 per cent around the mean'.

and again, he illustrates the vagaries of conventional tendering with the following

'Sets of drawings and documents were sent to a number of contractors for pricing. Some of the contractors received documents and drawings for the shell and main services for a repertory theatre; others received drawings and documents for a barn. The only difference between the sets of drawings and documents sent out was in name only, that of the label of the barn or theatre attached. Estimates for the theatres averaged £300,000, those for the barns £30,000. Unfortunately there were no funds available to test whether the barn would actually have cost £300,000 or the theatre £30,000'.

3. How can the estimator possibly relate his prices to reality when the following common system applies.

(i) A Bill of Quantities item is priced by an estimator, by relating this item to a similar item in a previous job and adjusting it according to the cost performance of that contract or tender. Of course, even if one started from a realistic base, this system is bound to become increasingly speculative as it departs from the original norm. If this seems rather harsh, we can refer again to Fine (1974) who makes the comment even more harshly.

'The method of selecting and placing contractors on tender lists, which is adopted by nearly all bodies letting contracts to the industry, ensures that no contractor is likely to get on more than one list in three, and that no contractor is likely to have fewer than five competitors in this list. This directly fragments the industry because no firm can expect to obtain more than 1/18 of the market, however good its performance.

Since we do not know how to bid more closely than within ± 10 per cent of overall cost, individual items in a Bill of Quantities must be priced at widely differing rates of different contractors. Indeed the rates in a Bill of Quantities containing several hundred items may be considered as random variates. In the author's experience, random values are quicker to generate and are indistinguishable from those generated by traditional techniques.

Estimating is like witchcraft; it involves people in foretelling situations about which they can have little real knowledge. There is some evidence to show that estimators escape from the real problems of their trade by presenting socially acceptable forecasts'.

(ii) When all of the items have been priced and a total reached, it is then sent to the Board for consideration who will then decide, according to circumstances, to increase or decrease the total, which completely upsets any reasoning in the original rates, even if there had been any such basis to begin with.

(iii) The prices will then very often be adjusted to account for this decision in such a way that those items most likely to become a factor in variations are priced high, whilst the others are priced low to compensate, making the total come out to the predetermined figure.

There are variations in this procedure and some contractual arrangements and Contractor's systems are a little more pure, but generally, this is the way the system works. That is not to suggest that Contractors are immoral or criminal in acting this way. They are merely operating a system.

4. There is the considerable time-scale which these non-creative processes demand. The preparation of the Bill of Quantities, and the process of tendering and evaluation can occupy between $\frac{1}{3}$ and $\frac{1}{2}$ of the pre-tender time on the shorter pre-contract periods.

5. The Bill of Quantities system provides no feed-back for the design team, nor is it a useful management tool for the Constructor. In spite of the time and care in preparation, the Contractor can only order materials from it at his own risk, and so in the main, he remeasures the work for ordering purposes. Very often, some of the work is measured even yet again for the final account involving resources for three measurements.

6. The language of the Standard Method of Measurement and the Bill of Quantities is not the normal language of the industry. In fact, apart from cost evaluation, the traditional Quantity Surveyor does not participate in the communication between designer and Contractor.

7. The Contractor cannot be part of the design team.

8. The present system gives no help for cost advice at the early stages of design.

9. The Contractor is often not provided with basic information, in many cases, essential to his price — e.g. names of nominated sub-contractors, permitted location of stores, etc.

The Merits of the Present System

1. It is an established and accepted system developed over 100 years.
2. The system has a reservoir of knowledge within itself which helps in a slow response time situation.
3. It has worked, by and large, to people's satisfaction for a long time.

The Demerits of the New Proposal

1. It could be argued that the scheduled items are limiting, although this need not be so.
2. The system has been proved, but is not widely known or understood.
3. It requires re-training and re-thinking in the industry.
4. Requires a motivating force sufficient to set up the system.

The Merits of the Proposal

1. The considerable gain in time.
2. Instant response to the design teams needs.
3. As later described, an opportunity for the Contractor to be brought into the design team, even before design commences.
4. Greater opportunity to provide data for cost planning.
5. Can be related to National cost indices.
6. Provides feed-back on performances with low response time.
7. Contractor is paid for work carried out — the speculative aspect of tendering is considerably reduced.

8. Rogue items do not exist because new schedule items can be made up from basic MpAMPI.

9. Substantial reduction possible in both tendering and construction cost.

The system could operate as follows. Contractors are supplied with a print-out of the unit schedules together with Materials, Plant and Manpower back-up, costs and sources, at any chosen interval but for the moment, say, monthly. That is to say, that the whole print-out is updated monthly from current information from a simple input. When a Contractor needs to be selected, which for the purpose of this description, is to be the one who gives the cheapest price for the work, a short list from the list of Contractors using the system will be selected. They would be supplied with the following minimum information:

(a) Site plan and location
(b) Size and type of contract
(c) Type of construction
(d) Start and/or completion date
(e) Special considerations

The list can be extended as desired, and can be sent out as soon as the client has committed himself to a project, or at any time thereafter up to the completion of the design.

Contractors will quote the percentage they require, above or below the rates that have been issued. This they can do within a week because in effect, the decision is now directly with the Board, without the preliminaries of preparing and pricing the Bills of Quantities. The successful Contractor will usually be the one who supplies the lowest percentage.

As the rates are maintained in an updated state, the percentage he gives will relate to the schedule as it exists at the tender stage. This obviates any risks for him being involved in inflation or deflation, because the percentage merely moves up or down with the rates. If the tender is fixed price, it will be fixed on the schedule operating at the tender stage. If it is fluctuating, then of course, the rise and fall in MpAMPI can be monitored by using the schedule, with or without indices, to give an instant final account.

Having established the chosen Contractor, his percentage is now given to data-store which is now in a position to give a current tender price figure for any item or items of work at any time. As these figures are available to the whole design system, they can be used for cost advice or in conjunction with symbols and blob quantities in the preparation of the design and tender on the drawing board.

If there are items in the building which are not in the item schedule, they can be easily made up from the basic MpAMPI plus the Contractor's percentage. This will be satisfactory, not only for the preparation of new rates, but for auditing variations to the contract and therefore rogue items can be eliminated. When the design is completed, data store or the computer, as the case may be, is requested to produce an immediate priced output which, if desired, can be in any one of the following forms:

(a) In trades — priced
(b) In trades — unpriced
(c) In network stages — priced
(d) In network stages — unpriced
(e) In sub-network stages — priced
(f) In sub-network stages — unpriced
(g) In functional groups — priced
(h) In functional groups — unpriced
(i) In sections (e.g. Blocks) — priced
(j) In sections (e.g. Blocks) — unpriced

Also priced advanced information schedules for suppliers and sub-Contractors as follows —

(a) In trades
(b) In network stages
(c) In sub-network stages

These are some of the possible print-outs, but of course the possibilities are considerable, and some possibilities which are less traditional and which make a real contribution to Design and Construction Management will be discussed in Chapter 6.

Before moving to the other aspect of Communication, i.e. that of Design Communication, it would be useful to assess the gains and losses to the Client/User and the design and construction team.

Client.	Any proposal which speeds the building process must be to his advantage if the penalties are not too great. He will know the tender cost of his project at an earlier date, and will be more likely to get the building he requires within an agreed budget. He can also have up to date monitoring information on progress and cost. He has nothing to lose and may also get some of the savings from reduced abortive costs.
User.	He is able to participate more easily in the design process, and the building he occupies should have a higher level of environmental evaluation as well as avoiding the last minute reduction of standards by cutting tender costs. He has nothing to lose.
Design Team.	Here there is something to lose. The Architect will fear that he may forfeit his freedom of design, and also fear that a more rigid management process will force a new pace or pattern of decision making. This is, however, a matter for him to decide in this proposed system, whereas other systems being brought out will not even give him that opportunity. The advantage of evaluation techniques are obvious. The Quantity Surveyor may fear what he has to lose, but in fact, he has a considerable amount to gain. There can be little dispute that the need for true building economics is acute. The present processes, not

only tie up quantity surveying resources in mundane tasks which prevent them filling these roles, but the tasks themselves devalue the profession. The Structural Engineer is furthest along the road of computer techniques and does not appear to have suffered. The Mechanical and Electrical professions are not likely to be dramatically affected and, in any case, have already become adjusted to computer operations, very often similar to the system proposed.

Contractor. Although he may see the biggest changes in the format of the information he receives, this should not represent a problem to him as the new form of data is compatible with his normal method of operation. He gains by a great reduction of resources, by avoiding abortive tendering processes, and also by becoming a member of the design team. He can also, under some circumstances, obtain better continuity of work with all that that entails. He has nothing to lose.

Apart from those who will always fear change of any sort, it is probably the Architect who has the most to fear although he may not be the one who objects the most, and in the long run may gain as much as anyone. The Architect's fear can probably be classified under two headings.

(a) Restriction of his design possibilities
(b) Restrictions on his ability to get the design implemented.

The first restriction has already been discussed, but the second can now be evaluated as the problems of design communication are considered and a proposal made for incorporation in the system. For this, it is again necessary to think of the fundamental needs, and try to ignore any tradition which may obscure the basic problem. As we have already seen, the problem of communicating design requirements does not occur when designer and Constructor are one and the same person. This applies to all forms of communication and not only those in the Construction Industry. The development of communication between people from the earliest time seems to have taken the form of both speaking and drawing. It is not important at this stage which came first, but this fundamental separation into two forms of communication is echoed in the development of computers. In this the development has been:

(a) Alphanumerics or the written word or coding,
(b) Graphics or the drawn sign or symbol.

In the case of early man's communication, the separation was slightly different because non-verbal communication was graphic, and only later did this become alphanumerics. The written and spoken language waxed over the centuries as the graphic representation waned. This has certainly been true since the invention of printing, until it reached the verbosity of Victorian prose. However, in recent years, the trend has very noticeably turned the other way; where the written word and the spoken word is becoming shorter and crisper, and graphics are used to speed the message.

There are probably several reasons for this, and these include films and television which make us more visually receptive. Also, the increased pace of society requires that the message is received as succinctly as possible. Examples of this trend are endless but a few may help to illustrate the point.

1.   An examination of cartoons over the last hundred years clearly shows how the Victorian cartoon would have an illustration with a long explanatory story below the picture, gradually the wording has reduced and the drawing has become more explicit, until today, there is often no explanation at all. The drawing itself contains a considerable amount of information which can be absorbed very quickly. The equivalent in word form would be lengthy. Trying to describe verbally to someone else a cartoon that has amused oneself illustrates this point very well.

2.   Television and other advertisements get over very long messages by using symbols representing characteristics which would otherwise take a long time to describe. This need for quick communication (apart from economics) may be due to our increasing urbanization, making us bored with long verbose presentations. Even professional firms tend to use their partners initials to create a quickly recognizable symbol.

3.   Necessity forces us to think graphically. A good example of this type of trend towards graphics is in road signs, where it is just not possible to read a long description at seventy miles per hour.

These are just some of the factors which are making us become extremely economic in our communication, and it is very sad to see that the Construction Industry is again going against the trend with ever-increasing documentation and verbalization.

In analysing the fundamental needs, there is obviously a choice of communicating non-verbal information by using either graphic or alphanumeric means and it is necessary to examine each on their own merits for the various tasks involved. For example, it would be possible to describe the directions for a long journey, but it would be quicker and easier to draw a map. Similarly, it is possible to describe a building by writing out coordinates, but it is obviously quicker and easier to illustrate shape graphically.

This may appear to be quite obvious, but the availability of equipment and materials often dictates or orientates the methods we use, rather than the truer way of analysing the task and developing the right equipment.

Computer equipment originally dealt with only alphanumerics, and even when graphics were developed they were more expensive and this caused a development of some architectural applications which input building shape by descriptions. Today, there is cheap graphic equipment as well as alphanumerics equipment and therefore the choice should be on the basis of the job to be done. Even in this improved environment, equipment is still too often chosen on the basis of cost. It may be worth recalling when making a choice of equipment, that a bicycle is cheaper than a motor vehicle, but this is no criteria when considering financial investment for say a delivery firm. Formal rules for the evaluation of the type of communication and equipment which should be used may not be possible, but at the very least, some guidelines can be established.

A drawing, in the context of building design and construction, is not only a means of transmitting spatial information, but is also important in the personal interplay between the designer and the drawing which has a considerable importance in the design process. Leonardo da Vinci in the following quotation shows how the creative mind obtains a stimulus.

'A WAY TO STIMULATE AND AROUSE THE MIND TO VARIOUS INVENTIONS

I will not refrain from setting among these precepts a new device for consideration which, although it may appear trivial and almost ludicrous, is nevertheless of great utility in arousing the mind to various inventions

And this is that if you look at any walls spotted with various stains or with a mixture of different kinds of stones, if you are about to invent some scene you will be able to see in it a resemblance to various different landscapes adorned with mountains, rivers, rocks, trees, plains, wide valleys and various groups of hills. You will also be able to see divers combats and figures in quick movement, and strange expressions of faces, and outlandish costumes, and an infinite number of things which you can then reduce into separate and well conceived forms. With such walls and blends of different stones it comes about as it does with the sound of bells, in whose clanging you may discover every name and word that you can imagine.'

Quoted McCurdy (1938).

In the same way, each line upon the paper helps to propose the next line and gradually a conversation is built up between the designer and the paper which is modified by the media and equipment. This modification of the design by media and equipment tends to be overlooked, but if for example a 4H pencil is used on a hard surface, a much tighter creative situation develops than when a 2B pencil is used on paper. In the last century, the need to use different materials at various stages of the process were well known, but these have now largely been forgotten. But these needs must be remembered if the product is not to suffer, for, as painters know, the size of the canvas and the type of brush have a significant effect on the painting.

Partly because the design professions in the Construction Industry have not interested themselves very much in Computer Aided Design, computer graphic equipment has largely been orientated towards industries where greater interest has created greater sales. Much of the existing computer graphics equipment is ideal for creating printed circuit designs, but is quite incompatible with the building designer's needs. Very often the equipment is based upon a glass tube, which is not only too small for the expansive thinking necessary for good design, but has the wrong sort of surface. The 'pen' is usually not a pen, but a photo-electric cell in the shape of a pen which because of its round glassy nature, slides over the glass tube without resistance. In addition, this tube is invariably placed in a vertical position, which not only creates problems of parallax, but is ergonomically quite incompatible with a designer's way of working. Fortunately, equipment is beginning to emerge which reduces some of these criticisms, but the situation does highlight the necessity for the requirements of the designer's equipment to be specified carefully; as the tools influence the product. So far, the fundamentals of two-dimensional drawing has been considered, but as previously discussed, there is the need to think and work in three dimensions. This can be done either by using working models or a computer, or a combination of both. There is a lot to be said for designing a building as a working model, which could then show up all those aspects of the problem which can cause irritation to the client, or confusion between members of the team. When the problem has been worked out in model form, it is very simple to translate this to the computer for processing. The alternative is to use a computer which can recognize the third dimension and this is now possible. Finally, one can use computer equipment to translate two-dimensional drawing into three-dimensional representations. Whichever form of input is used, it is almost certain that clients, users, and maybe even those responsible for development control will increasingly expect to see the three-dimensional effect of the spaces created. Legislation may well increase the emphasis upon the spaces between buildings, rather than the present emphasis on the elevational characteristics of individual buildings.

In any case, the advantages for the Constructor can be substantial. At the present time, production drawings are produced as a mean average of the needs of all those in the design and construction process. The conventional sets of drawings are probably not the Architect's ideal, almost certainly not the Quantity Surveyor's ideal and quite definitely not the Constructor's ideal. The reason for this is that one set of drawings is trying to provide for a wide variety of needs. The Architect needs to bring together as much generalized information as possible on to one sheet, so that the influence of one decision can be seen upon another. He will only layer this information on to several sheets when the first sheet becomes too confusing because of the amount of information being shown. These layers of information seldom relate to the construction needs on site, or even to the traditional taking off process for quantity surveyors. The greatest problem is no doubt for the Constructor, whose agent is faced with a formidable set of drawings which have to be correlated and understood almost instantaneously to enable ordering and work to commence. In addition, every time any activity is carried out, the relevant information will most likely have to be uncovered from several different sheets in a heap containing many scores of sheets. It is in this area that the computer can make a further significant contribution.

If the machine is adequately programmed, the Architect can put information into his drawing or graphic input in the way that suits him best, whilst at the same time, the output can be personalized to the needs of the other individuals in the team to whatever depth necessary, because the machine can reshuffle the information into differing arrangements. For example, outputs can be orientated to, say, the Quantity Surveyor, and at the same time orientated differently for the Contractor. Or the breakdown could be taken further so that each trade has its own print-out. These individual print-outs, together with the working model to help those on site to understand the total concept, can perhaps make a major contribution to productivity on site. Of course the same restructuring approach can be applied to both graphic and alphanumeric outputs. The machine is tireless, and can therefore keep reprocessing the data endlessly and usually at low cost. In the case of computer graphics, free and sketchy input drawings can be transformed into production drawings of the highest draughtmanship quality.

Machines using alphanumerics are usually more compatible with general usage in the construction industry because their needs in equipment terms are similar to any other industry. However it is probable that our ideas of letters and symbols and their presentation will change substantially, due to the influence of computers. Angular shapes are often used because all descriptions of shape emanate trom minimum coordinates. For example, a circle is made up of an infinity of straight lines, and therefore the instructions to a computer giving the coordinates would be impossible. Obviously the less instructions; the faster and cheaper will be the operation. This means that a square representing zero or a circle is more economic because only four coordinates are needed. This principle will apply until new methods are developed. The input of alphanumerics is usually by typing words, or codes for the words, into a terminal on what is, to all intents and purposes, a typewriter. The difficulty with using words is that this is very slow, and using codes is so boring and so difficult to remember that look up books have to be used, which again makes the job slow and laborious. Job satisfaction when using codes, is often lower than the job it is trying to replace, but, there is an alternative which is being investigated in Russia and America as well as the very useful work which has been done at the National Physical Laboratory. This is using a Palantype input. These typewriters such as seen in the House of Commons and American courts, have 29 keys which represent sounds rather than letters. This means that it is easy for an operator to take down even fast speeches at a slow typing speed, because each key represents a group of letters. It would seem possible that such forms of input could be developed for the Construction Industry to great advantage because the sounds are in effect translated directly into a code within the machine.

A combination of both graphic and alphanumeric input and output must be required in the Construction Industry, but it is hoped that the part which each will play will be evaluated against the real need, rather than chosen for expediency or initial cheapness. How both of these forms can be used to advantage must now be examined.

As a building is made up of the same basic functional parts within which there is a wide variety of alternatives, it might be possible to set up a library of symbols to represent the functional parts, and use alphanumeric suffixes to describe the type of infill within the functional group. An example of this is shown in the following illustration of how a space-divider symbol may be developed. Naturally, the way this would be used in present day computing is more sophisticated, but it does show the problem in its simplest form.

The symbols at the top of the illustration indicate the shapes which can accommodate any plan condition of a space-divider in a rectangular building. They do not relate to materials or components or shapes. If the data relating to a block wall, i.e. cost, weight, sound reduction, etc., is related

101

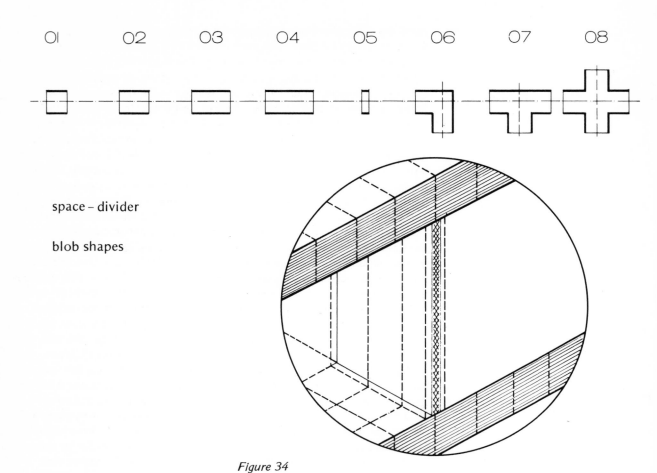

01 02 03 04 05 06 07 08

space – divider

blob shapes

Figure 34

to these symbols, then the computer will collect the symbols, and therefore the data, as the space-dividers are drawn on plan. Not only will the computer add together the information about the space-divider, but it will also deduct any necessary information from blobs already disposed. If the floor finishes had already been described in this illustration, then the area of flooring beneath the space divider would automatically be deducted. Similarly, for ceiling finishes, etc. Symbols can also be representative of three-dimensional space or even concepts which are particularly valuable when designing computer systems for traditional building systems.

Another example of this approach would be where a way through a space-divider or external envelope was needed as a basic function, the criteria could be given to data store or the computer, so that alternatives can be offered (functional group and criteria being specified). The criteria would include visual, thermal, aural and protection needs, amongst others. Because of the structure that has been proposed, the enquiry might promote offers, not only of doors, but also a heat curtain because this is a thermal solution for filling a void. It is worth noting that present data structures would not permit this cross-reference type of answer. Whichever option is

102

selected, it will fill a physical space in the building, and so the identification of the chosen item is made by a theoretical *'tick'* in the computer, related to function and position, which enables the computer to hold all the necessary information for transmission to the right person at the right time, without any use of codes at all.

Plotter drawings inform the Contractor where the items are to go, whilst print-outs will give him not only a specification, but names of suppliers and similar details. The system can be as lean or as comprehensive as desired, but whichever it is, there is no need for coding by human operators because it is the machine which, quite properly, handles the complex codes, whilst the designer is dealing with the functional criteria of his choice. As this approach can apply to all human activities, the location is the only problem not yet discussed and this can be handled perfectly well within the present dimensional co-ordination disciplines. A personal or office library of blobs of information needs to be built up, which must fit together pieces of data as though they were components of a building being assembled. There have been a lot of computer programs produced which have been concerned with the handling of graphic shape or volume which have been interesting, but they can have little value in the process unless they can contain all the information which is relative to them, and not only that of shape. Therefore we return to the need for theoretical spatial containers which can give shape to the building, and into these containers, items can be inserted according to their criteria. Just as the National grid referencing system enables any square metre of the United Kingdom to be identified and located; so can the Dimensional Co-ordination Standards be used to locate for the computer any of these containers or blobs. The computer theoretically identifies space in three dimensions for any chosen module. Therefore, by pointing to any particular square or cube, the location can be referenced. Running the pen along a series of grids gives lengths, or identification of four corners gives area, and so on. It can be seen that once a vocabulary of blobs was created, a building shape could be designed without materials being defined at all, and into which infills from the library can be placed. This would of course never be done, but illustrates the principles of the system which is remarkably similar to the traditional method of using a symbol for a brick wall; giving it length and height, and then deciding on the brick to be used. Each one of these containers or blobs must have the items in the library relating to it measured, so that the evaluative information which will be needed can be processed. In doing this, one should remember that the apparent precision of measurement is not precision at all, nor can it ever be, and that all measurements of building content are reasonable averages only. It would be impossible for every activity, material and its wastage, supervision, and so on, to be measured, and even if it were possible, a flu epidemic would make a nonsense of it all. At the moment there are wide disparities over the whole process between items which are measured with extreme precision, and those which are treated globally.

There are also large differences in the present measuring systems. The Electrical Contractor is usually asked to tender on the basis of conduit routes of his own choosing, but the Heating Contractor will be asked to price his tender on the basis of very rigid routing of water and other conduits. It is possible that the whole process could be improved by taking a more balanced view of measurement, but in any case, as this proposal's aim is to produce an integrated whole, it would be unreasonable to perpetuate the existing fragmented approach.

The electrical industry already have two major advantages in pursuing this proposed approach. They already operate systems whereby a symbol indicates the function, to which is added the description of the desired item to fulfil that function. The other advantage is that they, more than most, are given the design and performance criteria which they are then required to fulfil in the most satisfactory and economic way. It is this aspect which offers so much to the whole industry.

How would this approach affect COMMUNICATION? It has the effect of making the measurement of the blobs more average and less specific in the traditional sense, but at the same time much more precise in the sense that the criteria will be defined more precisely.

It is now possible to see how the whole Design and Cost Communication system can satisfy the required criteria.

1. Cost Communication advantages
(a) Enables a basis of cost and the identification of a Contractor to be established at a very early stage
(b) Economical use of resources
(c) Uses normal language of the industry
(d) Improved capacity for feedback of information
(e) Provides opportunities for total management system
(f) Allows for competitive tendering
(g) Allows normal conditions of audit and accountancy
(h) Gives improved design team potential
(i) Dramatically shortens the process
(j) Reduces the area of contractor's risk
(k) Reduces the contractor's waiting time for information on tender results

2. Design Communication advantages
(a) Personalized input and output of data
(b) Client/Users in a better position to participate in the design process
(c) The design team can work together with a reduced response time
(d) Dramatically shortens the process
(e) Boring and repetitive tasks are reduced
(f) Standards of production information raised
(g) Economy of resources

Finally, it is interesting to make a comparison of how this approach can compare with the times and processes indicated in the book on Develop and Construct, produced by H.M.S.O. for the Property Services Agency of the Department of the Environment. Please note that the P.S.A. proposed contract procedure for married quarters for the armed services assumes reduction of sketch plan time, whereas the computer can give increased design time and/or increased design analysis and evaluation support.

An Extract from PSA *Develop and Construct* is now given:

'The diagrams below compare the time-scale of a conventional contract with that of Develop and Construct. The feasibility stage has been omitted in each case but this does not invalidate the comparison. The great reduction in time expended by the Arcnitect's staff on sketch design and working drawings, combined with the overlap of Develop and Construct, results in the savings shown.'

Conventional contract: 46 months

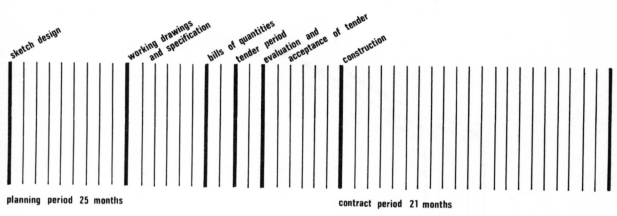

planning period 25 months   contract period 21 months

Figure 35

Develop and Construct: 34 months, saving 12 months

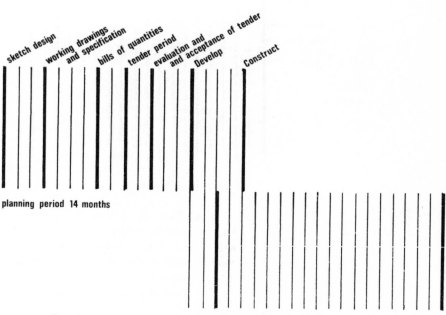

planning period 14 months

contract period 20 months

Figure 36

This highlights the position that in the CAD system shown below, the wasteful items such as tender period evaluation and acceptance of tender, etc., are carried out in parallel with Design, and not end to end. Working drawings, specifications and bills of quantities are replaced by an automatic processing system, giving the contractor, in addition, management information.

CAD: 22 months, saving over conventional contract 24 months (using similar criteria to those proposed for Develop & Construct)

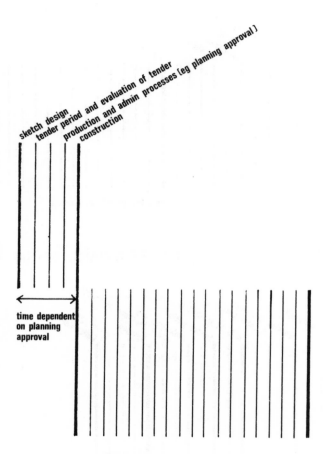

Figure 37

These charts are only shown for comparison with P.S.A. proposals, and are not meant to indicate an ideal programme of work which will be dealt with later. It is possible to reduce the CAD time still further, but there are good reasons for not cutting the design time which is already the area most often skimped and sacrificed to the other processes, even though it can have the greatest long term implications.

Chapter 6

CONSTRUCTION

The success or failure of a building contract is largely dependent upon the quality and timing of the information available. Although this may appear to be a truism, it is surprising how rarely a reasonable flow of good information is maintained throughout the team. There are a variety of reasons for this, and one is the very human fault of putting off decisions for as long as possible: particularly big ones.

One large organization carried out an experiment on this aspect of decision making by giving senior management a variety of decisions to make, ranging from simple to important and far-reaching. Fairly consistently, the small problems were dealt with and the decisions on the complex problems were delayed for as long as possible. The same pattern can be seen in the design and construction process. Another reason for poor information flow is often the lack of understanding of the problems of the other members of the team, which emanates from the compartmental and fragmented structure of the industry. It is almost inconceivable that an industry should still exist where the design process is completely divorced from the construction process, and furthermore, considered to be the right and proper system purely because of an administrative process to avoid collusion. Just because collusion is to be avoided does not prevent other industries from devising ways of integrating design and manufacture. How can there possibly be a proper basis for capital funding, purchase of and investment in equipment, and development of efficient processes, if the tendering system ensures that the Contractor can never know what the design team will produce next. Nor do they know what advantages the Contractor can offer, given the chance. It has been suggested that on the rare occasions where the Contractor has been brought into the design process, the results have been disappointing. But it can hardly be expected that the full fruits of such large scale operations could be observed in a short experiment because the Constructor, after so many years of being a passive receiver of information, will need time to adjust to becoming a contributor.

In order to evaluate the possible advantages of an integrated process, it might be worth examining the needs of the Constructor to see how far these have been satisfied by the present system, and how they might be satisfied in the proposed system.

The information needs of the Constructor (the man who builds) include details of ACTIVITIES to be carried out, from which he can obtain the types and quantities of MANPOWER needed, and he needs the quantities of MATERIALS and their location, from which he can establish PLANT requirements. He will require a programme and a sequence of activities which will enable him to establish when the men, materials and plant are required, and a management system to control cash flow and establish a final account. Included in this flow must of course be information for the sub-contractors and suppliers. The first thing that is clear is that the present systems are not orientated towards this situation at all, and, because of the failure of these systems to meet the Contractor's needs, they have become increasingly subject to change, and modifications have been proposed such as Elemental and Operational Bills of Quantities. The deficiencies of the present system are well-known and do not need to be defined here, but it may be worth noting that it 'gets by' because the cybernetical system has operated on a very slow response time which allows time for alterations, adjustments, and changes of mind. However, if the same system is speeded up, and a greater precision of information imposed, *the increased risk of claims must increase many times.*

In trying to analyse the requirements of a new system of output for the Contractor, it can be seen that he requires information to build, price, and finance the project, and that these revolve around a network of activities. Therefore let us see how far the information generated in COMMUNICATION can be applied to a network system, and what benefits might ensue.

For the majority of buildings, there is a limited range of network activities, which, whilst they may be changed in order, can largely be selected from a basic library of network stages. These stages can be identified by the Constructor and put together into the order in which he wishes to carry out the work. Also, the symbols and their quantities or blobs, created and positioned by DESIGN, can have pointers to their position in the network, i.e. a manhole symbol, once selected, would have its excavation, concreting and bricklaying allocated to each appropriate network stage. As each of these items is broken down within the computer into their MpAMPl characteristics, it is clear that each network stage will gradually gather all of the required Materials, Manpower types, Plant and Activity times for that stage, which can be given to the Constructor as individual or group print-outs. With the application of resource allocation network programs to this network, the Constructor is able to feed into the computer the resources he will make available, and obtain a length of contract because the Manpower types and their activity times are known. This process can be repeated until the desired balance between length of contract and available resources is established. When this is achieved, the Constructor can obtain print-outs showing the types and the quantity of MATERIALS, PLANT and MANPOWER, and when they will be required, which in turn can be translated into a cash flow chart for the project. All of this information, which is an automatic output from the Design process, truly forms the basis of a management system for the Contractor. So far, the word Constructor has been used as a description of the man who builds, and the word Contractor will be used for the man who embraces both construction and finance. It is perhaps unfortunate that the man who builds has become identified so closely with the profit aspects of the contract, and this has further confused the system. The Contractor's management accounting systems, which have so far been produced for computer operation have been largely divorced from the general information flow, but have become well developed and sophisticated in their own right. Because of this, and because the proposed system marries in very easily with these systems, they will not be dealt with in this chapter.

Where the two systems meet can probably best be illustrated in the following diagram.

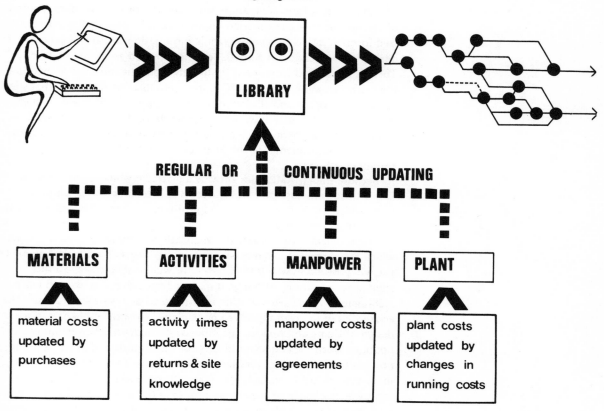

Figure 38

Ledger computer files for MATERIAL purchases; MANPOWER records for wages and salaries; PLANT records for amortization and hiring costs; all relate to the MpAMPI system. Bonusing can similarly relate to the activity file for both processing and updating. When these two systems are linked in this way, the contractor is able to identify his progress, profitability and future needs, at any time. He can also try different strategies, either before or during the contract, to test the effect of changing the level of resources upon his profitability.

As the same resource allocation management programs can be applied to the design process, the benefits of reviewing the whole process if the Constructor were to be brought into the design team must obviously be

109

substantial. Serial contracts, consortia, and other similar systems, often enable long term arrangements to be made with sub-contractors and supplier and in these cases, advanced information of probable demand can be sent out from the computer at the design stage, thereby enabling the period between final tender agreement and start of construction to be reduced to a minimum. All of these aspects contribute towards shortening the response time and therefore shortening the whole process.

As discussed in the previous chapter, the computer is able to reconstitute the information put in by the design team into a variety of different forms for the Contractor. Information documented under MpAMPI headings, or in a form compatible with, say, the British Standard Method of Measurement or any other arrangement, can be provided in a personalized form. Similarly, drawn or graphic information which will generally deal with the location of activities can be provided according to need. There is a real need for research in this area, but the information within the machine can be 'bundled', if desired, into locational areas so that site operatives have at hand all the information required in that area, rather than searching through drawings of the whole contract, or constantly returning to the site hut for information. Sortations can also be supplied for making adjustments for the final account according to the NEDO formula method.

Because the MpAMPI files provide a platform which is being kept in line with current costs, the Contractor is able to concentrate on those items which affect management and profitability, and therefore he is able to contribute to Design.

The problem is to evaluate the implications of simple design decisions which are at present taken in isolation by the designer. With time an expertise will grow up in which the Contractor will be able to make a substantial contribution. Although it may be feared that this will influence architecture, this is after all what architecture has always been about. The economics of excavation, as we know, played a considerable part in the design of Georgian London. The Modern Architectural Movement could not have taken the course it did without the invention of manufacturing processes which enabled very large sheets of glass to be produced. It is more than probable, in fact, that it was the potential of such large glass areas which stimulated creative architects in the way Leonardo da Vinci described. It is possible that a new relationship of the design and construction team, together with the potential of the computer, might act as a similar stimulus to an industry which currently lacks any of the crusading spirit that it had in the recent past? The Contractor will have to make a contribution to the economics of production which will be covered by the percentage he gives as an addition, or reduction, to the MpAMPI rates. Clearly this percentage would increasingly be seen to reflect his management ability and therefore his efficiency. It is true that this percentage also includes for those items which cannot reasonably be included in the schedules, but as these are common to all tenderers, the issue increasingly becomes one of efficiency, which is not necessarily reflected in the present system. Experience shows that more and more items, at present included as preliminaries, can be converted to measured rates as users become accustomed to the approach, and this means that the percentage becomes purer.

It is immaterial whether the Contractor is a direct labour force, package dealer, or operating the conventional contracting organization, because these are only administrative arrangements which do not affect the basic functional and modular approach.

However, the social factors which will affect the administrative and organizational arrangements cannot be ignored, because they will have a serious effect even upon the conventional processes.

The industry, because of its centuries-old background of art and craftsmanship which could exist on low capital investment, is finding difficulty in adjusting to a new financial situation, and this is aggravated by the separation of design and construction. One only has to imagine any other large industry operating in this way to understand the problem. Supposing cars, clothes, household goods, etc., were designed individually and sent out for competitive tender, would it be possible to set up the production processes and find the capital for such investment as seen in those industries today? It may be argued that that is what industrialized building is all about, but there are differences. The Construction Industry suffers from the continuous stop-go policies of successive governments, and now in fact seems to accept this as a norm. But of course, it is difficult to persuade people to increase capital investment in a process which behaves in this way. Equally, because it is a disparate, disunited and low capital industry, it is easier politically to cut it back than for instance the motor industry, where repercussions are immediately fed back to government through trade unions and capital. The one influences the other. This, added to the historic background of low experience, means that prefabrication and industrialized building systems have not, like other industries, always learnt the problems of investment, amortization, and so on. This means that the pricing of the systems is invariably too high because of trying to pay off overheads too quickly, and this in turn means lower demand, and so on. This has been aggravated by them suffering from payments being made as though the buildings were traditional, with the consequent effect on cash flow. If payments were made on the supply of materials to the factory as if it were a site, costs could again be reduced.

It has also been possible for the Contractor to avoid the responsibilities of design by leaving this, the greatest risk, with the design team who are probably least able to carry the risk, except by indemnity insurance. A somewhat bizarre situation. When the industrialized builder has tried to overcome some of these problems, he has invariably made two basic mistakes which in the end become critical. Firstly, he has economized on the design costs. It would seem extraordinary, but many system builders use the cheapest technical labour they can get for design, probably because of a lack of understanding of the problem, which thereby creates an alienation of the product with the client who in many cases could, or should, be a well-qualified man. Secondly, once having found a design which sold, he persisted with the same design for year after year until the disenchantment with the design became identified with the manufacturer. This fault, unfortunately, even befell most local authority consortia building where, *to the public eye*, the buildings looked the same over periods of ten to fifteen years. This is undoubtedly not acceptable to the public taste even if they were 'one off' designs. They may look different to professionals, but not to the lay observer. Again, there are exceptions to these criticisms, but it is significant that, in general, it is the exceptions which have proved to be successful. From this one can see that a higher level of investment in the industry will have to be considered, which in turn will have an effect on the relationship of the team. If the design team are incorporated into a total package there is the problem that invariably occurs where the designs become 'unlively' because the team ages, systems build up which act as cushions against change, and so it goes on. On the other hand, the problems of keeping the design and construction apart are plain to see. The proposed system does at least offer, through the computer, the opportunity to get the best of both worlds, and thereby the designer and constructor can work together but are not irrevocably tied to each other for all time. The similarities with other industries can readily be seen.

These new arrangements of the team must inevitably raise the question of supervision of the contract, which was touched upon in the last chapter. Supervision, like most of the processes in the building industry, has some very odd imbalances, again no doubt, due to tradition remaining in a process which has undergone change. It is normal for items such as the making of concrete to be watched and tested to a considerable degree by an agent of the client during its manufacture on site. So long as the hours of work of the person so delegated coincide, the process will be carefully monitored, but, during holiday periods, sickness etc., the level of supervision invariably drops, and the degree of trust in the Contractor rises. Furthermore, those items manufactured off site will be taken at face value, particularly as today, they arrive more and more in a pre-packaged condition. Sometimes a pre-cast unit will be smashed at random, but this can only rarely be done because of the impact upon production. Other items such as drains, heating, and electrical systems, are watched by a substantial number of supervisors even though much of it is never seen, which, on the final test often shows up grave deficiencies. Yet, in spite of the watching and testing of *in situ* parts, other components such as refrigerators, cooking equipment and an increasing array of complex equipment are installed without test. If 'switching on' is good enough for the complex items, why is it not good enough for the *in situ* items? It will be argued that the *in situ* items are an integral part of the structure and cannot be easily replaced, but that also applies to the pre-manufactured components which are accepted as a whole. Local authority consortia have tried to overcome this problem by sending Clerks of Works to the suppliers to check manufacture of such items at random, but of course the proportion inspected must inevitably be small. There is also of course the legal implications of the client's agent possibly watching the installation of faulty products, which can become acute as the number of off-site manufactured goods increase. In the present process it is difficult to formulate a good and simple solution to the problem, but in the proposed system where it is possible for the Contractor to become a member of the management and design team with his profit or management fee related to efficiency, it may well be that a new relationship will emerge similar to that which occurs in any other industry, i.e. the Contractor will be responsible for the finished product. If the design team, including the Contractor, are able to be more precise in their needs, then the Contractor, as manager of the construction process, will be able to take the responsibility for producing the right job at the right time. Furthermore, the design team should have more time to examine and understand the site and manufacturing process and avoid the wasted time in site meetings which are very often taken up with problems which are not the concern of the design team in the true sense. Site meetings are sometimes thought to give practical experience, but in fact, usually fall far short of this ideal.

At the present time, there is a serious situation whereby parts of a relatively fixed labour force are drawn from one Contractor to another according to successes and failures in the tendering game. Because of the low response time, this is aggravated as it is difficult for Contractors to keep labour continuity which often has to be maintained at the expense of the client's completion dates, or start dates, or both.

If local, regional or national MpAMPI centres were set up, then the response time being reduced to almost nothing, together with the better evaluation of resources, would enable work within the Industry to be better balanced, thereby giving a better opportunity for continuity. That is not to say that conventional systems with unpriced Bills of Quantities cannot be used within the system and in parallel with other forms of tendering.

Two things emerge from the analysis so far which are of particular importance to Contractors:

1. The development of such processes would change his role. At present he is a passive recipient of instructions, with flexibility only to decide a mode of operation within very severe limits. And yet he is the one who should have the greatest expertise in constructional techniques and methods. The problems of construction management and site labour organization is not part of the design team's concern in this industry. Whilst this situation will not, and cannot continue in any case, the new proposal allows a reasonable relationship between design and construction whilst safeguarding the client's interest, which other systems may not provide. New systems are certain to emerge for one reason or another, because, in particular, overseas contracts, where homegrown systems are re-evaluated, have created an atmosphere in which consortia, consisting of design teams, Contractors and quite often sub-Contractors as well, have been set up. In these consortia, the Architect very often does not occupy his traditional role as the instigator of the process. Quite often, the Contractor, and sometimes even a sub-Contractor such as an air-conditioning firm, can be the initiator who selects his consultant, rather than the other way around. These influences will no doubt affect processes in the domestic environment where tradition plays a larger part.

2. The other effect upon the Contractor will be the possible re-examination of the benefits, or otherwise, of industrialized building, or even what is meant by the term. It is obvious that every single building, no matter how traditional it may appear, contains a large proportion of industrialized building components, or in other words, those made in a factory off-site. It is equally obvious that even the most industrialized building system has a certain amount of traditional site operations. At what point does traditional building become industrialized building, or prefabricated building as it was

once called? The answer would appear to be not the degree to which the factory made components are used, but the level at which design, particularly external appearance, is constrained. The Contractor will therefore have to recognize the balance between the capital investment in plant and equipment, related to the design life of the product. Even in the Georgian, Victorian and suburban phases, each standard design at some time caused a reaction. The process in architecture does not appear to be dissimilar from that in other products in that there is an initial resistance to the new design, followed by general acceptance and fashionability, followed by violent reaction for at least one generation. It may be argued that to consider architecture in this light is incompatible with that which we hold most dearly in the environment, but that would be hypocrisy.

The following factors might be considered:

(a) A viewpoint might be that the built environment is too precious for us to use mass-production techniques. Clearly, this was not thought so by the builders and purchasers of the houses in Georgian and Victorian suburbs, and suburbia of the 1930's, where vast areas of land were covered with identical house designs and built on a production line process which probably reached its ultimate in the Levitt towns of America. However, much of that which is over 40 years old is now rated highly as part of our heritage.

Not only this, but we have incorporated large car parks into our urban environment which are covered with industrialized spatial units; known as cars, which are produced to a limited range of designs. The rural scene has a rapidly expanding area of land, very often in the most popular scenic areas being covered with caravans and mobile homes and which are fully industrialized products. We do not stop the mass production of these units with their impact on the environment. Indeed, the legislative requirements of these products are considerably less than for those of conventional building. Already, about 130,000 people live permanently in this type of building, on over 5,500 registered sites in the U.K. alone. This is apart from the vast numbers of caravans (designed without controls) which obscure the elevations of an equally large number of houses which have gone through incredible feats of aesthetic control.

(b) Another viewpoint might be that industrialized building had a lower standard than traditional building. In the absence of any known survey it is impossible to make a judgement. The only view that one can propose is that generally, the public and the user is more satisfied with industrialized building than most traditional designers.

Denigration of post-war industrialized building has invariably come from the professions, rather than the users, who on the whole, appear to be remarkably satisfied with the products. Neither traditional building nor prefabrication can claim a very high record of postwar popularity of performance either in the fulfilment of functional needs or cost in use.

(c) Industrialized building costs more than traditional building. This is a commonly held view. Apart from the fact that this is only partially true, the major reason for this is the lack of understanding of capital investment as explained above. Also, it is often assumed that the fall in price by manufacturing increasing numbers of the same product proceeds as an infinite decline. Clearly, there must be a cut-off point if the product isn't to eventually cost nothing, and this cut-off point depends upon the product under consideration. The mechanics of establishing these cut-off points in production are well known, but the dissemination of this information to the design team is virtually unknown. This is critical, because by using these platforms there can be a reduction in the amount of boring repetition, with an increase in job satisfaction, without loss of profitability. The computer could not only help to evaluate the economic production levels, but also provide feedback information to the design team. The techniques for this approach are being developed in other industries and should be developed in the building industry.

Irrespective of whether building is totally industrialized or not, the economic balances which affect the sub-Contractors and Suppliers cannot be ignored by the design team. In the traditional situation the Contractor would buy material almost on a day-to-day basis and the manufacturer would only be required to hold small stocks, which in turn meant that only small quantities of capital were held in stock. When the scale of the problem increases, other factors begin to emerge. For example, the design team may seek low cost with maximum variety of components, but this means that the manufacturers must maintain large stocks if a quick 'call off' is required. This in turn affects the financial standing of the manufacturer and if the variety demand becomes excessive, it reflects back upon the price which can lead to a drastic reduction in choice. The problem varies according to the type of process and the type of material used. Plastic foams, for example, can be made quickly to order and only require small stocks to be held, whereas steel components with low response time and wide variety, can involve very considerable capital investment. These problems are well known to the Contractor, but because of the nature of the industry are often virtually unknown to the design team who create the market. Work has already been carried out by Local Authority consortia to a sufficient degree to establish the direct interaction between the selection of components by the design team and the production processes, by using communication by computer. These and other aspects may force the industry into a choice between a system using a maximum variety of building components adminstered by sophisticated computer systems, or to a limited range of cheap components which will involve only comparatively small quantities of tied up capital in unordered stock. Whichever the direction the industry takes, it will be impossible in the future for the design team to isolate themselves from the effects of these factors on the manufacturing processes.

Architects and the other members of the team have come to recognize the problems of cash flow within their own offices and therefore have some respect for these problems, but as yet, there is not the same understanding of the problems of labour resources. One of the Contractor's major problems is to make the most efficient use of labour against a background of trade unions and legal requirements. The design team, because the information is largely denied to them, ignore the effects of their decisions on labour resources and concentrate on costs. A request to a Quantity Surveyor is always for an estimate of cost and not of resources, as it is assumed that the one reflects the other. This is of course not true. One choice may be cheaper but longer in activity time, which in the long term can turn out to be a very expensive alternative for the client. None of the design team are to blame as it is the system that does not provide for the feed-back of this type of information. Not only is this risk reduced when the Contractor becomes part of the design team, but because the activity time is attached to each symbol, an evaluation of labour resources can be made at any time. The proposed system gives an opportunity for the design and construction team to work together and for each to make his own contribution. If this is done, there is hope that together, a satisfactory and common solution to the problem of integrating the client/user might become possible by reducing the response time and increasing the communication flow. The alternative is fairly certain. The Contractor, because of his financial strength, will increasingly produce building systems for the general field of architecture, which will become more and more attractive to the client because of cost and time benefits, and which, in the long run will be stimulated by advertising and the offer of maintenance agreements to be discussed in the next chapter.

Even in a stringent economic environment the professional man and the Contractor maintain a competitive situation at arms length, whereas they are in a true symbiotic situation, because if either goes down, the other must go down too.

Chapter 7
MAINTENANCE

The number of organizations which adopt a comprehensive and positive attitude to Maintenance Management are unfortunately still extremely small, but for most of building there is no normal provision for maintenance at all. This is surprising, because the effects of maintenance and cost in use are of profound significance to all, and particularly to those in control of large building resources. The techniques and the knowledge is well developed, but the building owners and the design team have, apart from the energy crisis which drove the point home, taken little interest in the subject. Cuts in the capital cost of buildings are invariably made at the expense of cost in use, whilst the staff employed in maintenance management usually have little influence in management. Yet, the effects of running and maintaining a building can be infinitely more significant over a sixty-year period than the capital cost, as can be seen in the following analysis for an old people's home in Shoreham, Sussex.

Capital cost (final account)	4.80 %
Fees:	
Architect	
Q.S.	
Consultants	0.59 %
Loan charges	
Initial furniture and equipment	94.61%
Approx. gross annual running costs (60 years)	
	100.00 %

Based on estimate of total costs over a period of 60 years excluding inflation or changes in value of building.

It is often thought to be good business to try and economize on design fees, but this analysis shows that a poor design team in a hurry could aggravate the gross annual running costs, but a cut in their fees would barely be perceptible. It is not just a question of designing to save energy or even to reduce the painting of buildings, but consideration must be given at the design stage to all aspects of the cost in use of buildings. The internal cleaning, walking distances and so on must all be taken into account. Those associated with hospital design have probably been more aware of these problems than most, but in general, the problem is again one of poor communication flow.

This communication flow can again be improved by incorporating the appropriate feed-back information into a computer based data system. Energy requirements can be tested simply and precisely at the design stage as already explained. Areas which require painting for example, either inside or outside, have their MpAMPI characteristics available to the design team so that at the design stage the labour resources for decoration can be estimated. Areas of floors and walls and their finishes can be collected for evaluation of cleaning costs, and print-outs can be obtained for maintenance agreements. Items which are covered by guarantees and insurances, or which are cyclical can have 'bring forward' notices in the machine.

If the maintenance records are processed by computer, then records of failures can be conveyed automatically to the materials and component selection file, so that the level of its performance can be assessed at the time when the designers make a choice. With this approach, it is hoped that Maintenance and Cost in Use will be established as a function in the process which requires proper management representation brought into the Design process at the appropriate time. However, this is only one aspect of maintenance records: that of feed-back to the designer. There are others.

The overall supervision of a large number of projects can cause difficulties, and the scale and scope of the problem varies enormously. Large Local Authorities and Government departments, for instance, control so many buildings and sites which are continuously being bought and sold, that a full record of their ownership at any one time is difficult to maintain by manual processes. Even when they are complete, they are usually extremely difficult to handle because most of the information is kept in traditional files with poor cross-referencing. The forms of records for various items have usually been developed on an *ad hoc* basis by each section, and these provide little compatibility one with another. The bases for measurement, for example, are often difficult. A simple item such as area can be described in a variety of ways. Costs are quite often based upon area within the external walls, including area of partitions; but areas for cleaning are within the external walls, but excluding area of partitions. Areas for heating would be based on temperature zones, and so on.

It is accepted that each of these types of calculations are required, but it is essential for communication accuracy that each is allocated its proper place. All too often it is not clear what is being discussed, and this, together with the other facets of data collection, make the risks of bad communication very high. It is comparatively simple to avoid this problem, and at the same time provide a data base for evaluations.

Firstly, it is necessary to agree the standards by which maintenance records will be kept and criteria be measured. This can often be done by getting a copy of all the forms used, and rationalizing them. Implementation can best be achieved by withdrawing the old forms and replacing them with the new forms. If agreement can be reached on standard positions for information, these can even be read automatically by computer through optical reading devices, thereby obviating the need for laborious inputs. Once the standards have been agreed the rest is easy, because very quickly, by normal administrative processes, a great fund of information starts to collect. Data Store creates a structure for this data which will enable the following types of examinations to take place.

A simple enquiry through a video terminal attached to a computer which has been programmed as suggested, can bring forward a variety of types of information. The whole list of projects can be examined. If there are so many that they more than fill the screen, they can be examined as if pages were being leafed through. Alternatively, buildings can be brought forward by district, location, or criteria. These criteria could be for age, or building type, or constructional type, or fuel usage, and so on *ad infinitum*. If desired, more than one criteria can be used. The process is exactly the same as that proposed for the Materials File. A project, or projects, are located by entering the criteria and the computer makes the sortation. If all the details on one project are required, then this too can be given.

In the case of location, if the search area is substantial, this can be done as follows:

Using a grid system such as the Ordnance Survey Geocode reference, which consists of a twelve-figure code for the identification of any one square metre of the United Kingdom, this can be translated into a simple location system in which the user does not recognize that he is handling twelve-figure codes at each stage. The basic system gives references in an easterly direction and in a northerly direction. By showing a drawing of, say, England on a video screen which has, superimposed upon it, this grid system, the user points to the square in which he is interested, which is then replaced by a magnification of this same area and again with a grid, he identifies the square in which he is interested and so on, until he gets down to the level of detail he seeks, which can if required be the identification of any one square metre.

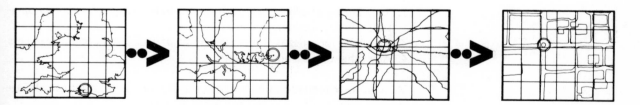

Figure 39

Each square in the grid now becomes a container of information like a blob, and, as explained in the next chapter, can be related to the meteorological file already held in Data Store, as well as information on population, ownership, etc.

Another valuable search technique which can be used in maintenance and cost in use, is that of fuel economy. If each building is kept on file, the required details of that building will also be held. At the design stage of a job, a heat loss calculation and its consequent conversion through the type of heating system used and the fuel to be used, is a comparatively normality, but at present, when this is done, this estimated fuel consumption is unfortunately put into a file and never looked at again. If this figure were to be put into the project computer file, it could be called up at any time for comparison with the actual fuel consumption. Running through a list of projects, no matter how long it may be, those consumptions which show a great disparity can be identified, and these can be investigated. A further sophistication is of course to relate the computer accounting system for the payment of bills to this system, so that monitoring becomes semi-automatic. This is only one of the many examples of building maintenance criteria which can be examined in this way, providing additional staff resources for considering maintenance surveying in a positive manner, instead of the rather traditional passive approach of reacting to troubles after they have occurred, rather than seeking out potential difficulties before they occur.

Other possible entries to the file can be seen in the maintenance handbooks such as that published by the R.I.B.A. The value of such information as this, is that re-ordering of broken components can be simplified by relating maintenance records to the original materials file which holds component numbers, names and addresses of manufacturers, and suppliers. In the traditional system, the information is usually somewhere within the organization, but because of a lack of structure in the information, very often cannot be found and so a search is started from scratch, with all the time that that involves.

A computer diary system, which can be so useful throughout the system can again be employed here. The computer holds a diary for many years ahead and is able to accept requests against this diary, so that reminders or automatic print-outs are produced on the chosen date. The following are some examples of the type of information which might be found useful to put on such files:

1. End of guarantee reminders.
2. Re-painting schedules and specifications to be brought forward automatically for inspection.
3. Reminder for renegotiation dates for maintenance and other agreements.
4. Any other cyclical arrangements.

Many of these reminders which relieve the pressure on Maintenance Management can actually be initiated at the design stage.

Even the basic MpAMPl system can be of considerable assistance to Maintenance, because exactly the same process can be adopted as those for tendering procedures. As has already been mentioned, the Property Services Agency already produces schedules of rates for minor works and maintenance of roads and pavings, which could form the basis for such a system. It might be argued that any one organization does not handle sufficient maintenance to make such a proposal viable, but voluntary grouping of such requirement for common benefit can be done.

For example, a system of this kind is in operation in France where the Confédération de l'artisanat et des petites enterprises du bâtiment (CAPEB) has set up five regional SARTEBs (Services artisinaux de répartition des travaux d'entretien du bâtiment) which centralize the demand for maintenance work and distribute it between member firms of craftsmen. They also carry out cost assessments and handle payment.

These types of systems, therefore, need not only apply to large organizations maintaining their own buildings.

In any case, as with most areas of the industry, significant changes are likely to occur. The problems of finding resources, with its subsequent effect on cost, in a situation where the stock is increasing, but the labour force is decreasing, must become more and more acute particularly with an increasing demand for conservation of buildings absorbing traditional trades. So much so in fact, that there is likely to be a growing pressure on the maintenance of buildings being linked to the construction contract. Just as the purchase of most major products is influenced by the manufacturer's ability to provide a good maintenance service, so may be the choice of building construction or Contractor. Certainly, industrialized building systems, in the future will be sold with maintenance agreements, and it is likely that other building users will go to central building maintenance consultants. Even at present, there are a considerable number of unco-ordinated maintenance services for the various parts of a building such as lifts, cooking equipment, computer equipment, air conditioning, etc.

It is surprising that a client will employ design consultants for substantial fees, go through elaborate tendering and Contractor selection processes and yet, sometimes even before the building has been completed, employ an assortment of firms in a quite arbitrary manner to carry out alterations and maintenance. Often, the work is done quite indiscriminately and with no reference to the original design philosophy, and in these cases, can sometimes cause a capital depreciation. These same building owners would probably never dream of adopting the same methods with their cars. It is not only the ignorance of the building owner, but sometimes the indifference of the design team which aggravates the problems of maintenance and for this, changes may have to be considered. Before this is done, it is worth recalling an incident to illustrate the need for the monitoring and maintenance of building being fed back to the design team.

A primary school at Eastergate in Sussex, which had been designed with fixed windows and a controlled ventilation system (not air conditioning) was being very heavily monitored. Air temperature, air movement, humidity and many other environmental factors were being monitored by computer and manual means. There was almost complete satisfaction with the building from the users but there was one persistent complaint, namely, that one room felt airless, and staff and pupils became sleepy. But repeated and careful examination of all the records could not suggest any physical deficiency. The normal reaction would have been to call in a local builder to put in an opening window which would have unbalanced the rest of the school. However, as the building had been so carefully monitored, the Consultant Engineer looked further and suggested the replacement of an acoustically absorbent ceiling with a hard ceiling, whereupon, with the installation of the new ceiling, the complaints stopped. The problem was one of acoustical deadness and not one of airlessness.

This example illustrates a situation where totally incorrect action is often taken in building maintenance which is based upon:

(a) lack of monitoring,
(b) lack of knowledge because of lack of monitoring,
(c) the client not using the expertise of the original design team.

If we are to conserve not only existing stock, but stock which is yet to be built, changes will have to come.

Education will have to play its part in showing the need for:
(a) bringing the maintenance managers into the design process,
(b) providing more opportunities for training in maintenance management so that it is able to play its part,
(c) the design team to be made aware of its responsibility for its design, even after it has been completed, and
(d) the building owners to be made aware of the losses they suffer at present and those losses that are yet to come, as well as the gains they could make.

This must not only apply to the buildings, but also to their surrounds. It is sad, but all too commonly one sees a building which has been rationalized to reduce site labour, being surrounded by labour intensive site works such as cobbles. Other buildings, which are so-called functional are often surrounded by the most incredible and difficult to maintain paths, pavings and flower beds. Landscape Architects advice must be sought at the design stage on layouts, which should facilitate maintenance and probably reduce first cost, as well as maintenance cost.

A greater integration between the users, maintenance management and the design team must not be seen to be just another drain upon the design team's time, but a real need, and a satisfying job.

One of the most satisfying aspects of building design is the rapport that can be obtained with the user, and which can be reflected in the continuing care and appearance of a building because he trusts the designer, and seeks his continuing advice. This aspect will be returned to later because it reflects a design attitude which is important to the process, as well as affecting information methods. So far as maintenance management is concerned, computer aids can be made available to facilitate not only its own work, but also its contribution to the design of buildings.

Chapter 8
POLICY

What is POLICY, and why should it come at the end? Because the design and construction process is a continuous spiral, which has to be cut at some point to establish a starting point for a description of the information flow, a decision on the position of the cut must inevitably be fairly arbitrary. Any organization, whether large or small, must have a policy, and this is best established after an examination of the problem, which has, to some degree, been carried out in the preceding chapters. A policy can only be established against the view of future events, which in itself represents a hypothesis and which again, as we have seen, is born of ANALYSIS — SYNTHESIS — EVALUATION, i.e. the same activity as Design, or any creative activity.

In the case of POLICY, a plan for the future is created for present use, subsequently to be amended and eventually to be discarded. This activity is often considered to be a luxury in the humdrum of rushing from crisis to crisis, but if the process is rationalized, time can be found to look ahead and to consider the reasons which cause an uneven work flow, amongst other things.

The first reason is that the structure of the industry is so fragmented, and the second is the fact that world wide, the industry is used as a political tool and an economic regulator.

Whilst it is recognized that all industry must be subject to some degree of economic and political pressure, the Construction Industry seems to have become a particular target, and this has made it weak; and because of its weakness, a likely target for further pressures. This cycle must be reversed in order that the industry may gain strength to withstand these pressures, and this is not impossible. With an undoubted future world demand, the industry has to concentrate on being strong, economic, and efficient, and for this a scenario is required for the future, together with a policy of how this can be achieved.

A view of the future, with its constant re-evaluation, is important because:

(a) It is important as a motivation and direction for everyone in the organization.
(b) It is important because nothing stays the same and therefore we must look for future change
(c) It is important to re-evaluate the organization's (whether small or large) position in this changing situation.

It is unfortunately true that many keen efficient and industrious organizations have often worked so hard that they have looked up to find themselves bankrupt, purely because they have not noticed the continuously changing environment in which they work. No matter how much one may wish otherwise, the world will continue to change as it always has done.

To survive in this evolutionary situation, there must be a part of the organization which can foresee change, not only in the product, but also in its own organization, and this requires a management structure. Before considering this structure, it would be useful to reconsider some aspects of the environment in which it will operate.

1. Design

From time to time, it is necessary to reconsider what one means and feels about design rather than just mouthing the words. Some peculiar anomalies in our views of art have already been discussed in earlier chapters, but there are a great many more areas which need to be examined and thought about, if the industry as a whole is to make a proper contribution to society. Of these, the one which is critical to any plan for the future is that of user participation. This raises a critical issue which must be openly and honestly discussed; of how personal is an act of creation, and how can a designer work in an environment of user participation. Already there are signs of strain and anxiety about this relationship which is hardly surprising, as the problems of working in multi-disciplinary teams hasn't yet been fully resolved. Will the designer persuade himself that what he (the designer) wants, is what he (the user) wants, and the better he is at selling his ideas, the more successful he will be? Or will he wait to be told by the user what to do? This may sound rather absurd, but seen against the problems of multi-disciplinary team working, we can hardly be smug about the problem. Are we to return to a Renaissance situation where special buildings are designed according to one man's 'flash of inspiration' and the remainder to be designed pragmatically and collaboratively between design team and user? Has any one man the right to impose his 'flash of inspiration' on others, or can it be justified as spiritually uplifting?

2. Construction

Most smaller contractors recognize, for a large number of reasons, that the future is unlikely to make it possible for them to carry on in their present way; but they are tied to a professional system which provides most of the work. Neither one recognizes their symbiotic situation. Small professional offices and small Contractors have far more in common with each other than they have with their big brothers in their own fields, and yet to have a Christmas drink together raises suspicions of collusion. Why is this? Could one feel confident in an aeroplane if one knew that the designer was prohibited from talking to the Contractor or Constructor during the design? This attitude can only be attributed to the tendering system we have developed. The industry must surely become a cohesive unit with different methods of accountability.

3. Management

The last two considerations raise the third which is whether existing management structures can continue against this background of potential change.

primitive
no
organization

agrarian
pyramid
organization

technological
group
organization

Figure 40

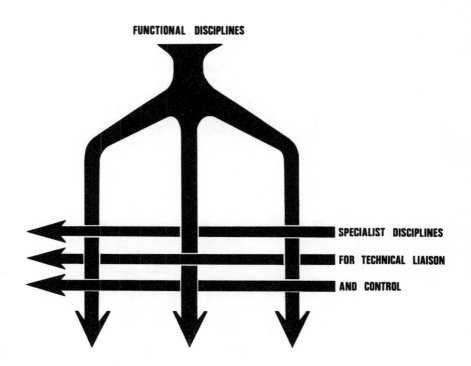

Figure 41

Over the last two thousand years, there has been a continual trend for the hierarchical pyramid to become flatter and flatter (Figure 40). These changes can be seen in many walks of life, but probably best illustrated in the armed services. In the early basic situation, and up to a hundred or so years ago, the pyramid was steep and the procedures were simple and well-known throughout the pyramid. The simple processes were understood by man and General alike, and reinforced by repetitive and intensive training. The General at the top of the pyramid not only understood the mechanisms of the command he was giving, but also knew that it would be properly translated right down to the recipient of the instructions. The commands were limited to a few well-drilled movements. It is only in comparatively recent times that new and different problems have begun to emerge, and these again follow the same pattern as those in the Construction Industry. The difference that has emerged is that, not only the General at the top cannot understand the whole process, but neither can the intermediates or even those on the same strata. The military services overcame this problem in the early stages by a clever manoeuvre. They formed a matrix style of management (see Figure 41).

A very good system based upon a warp-and-weft style of management, which can be valuable for the Construction Industry. However, as more and more sophisticated systems are used, this leads to loose knit teams of specialists put together for a particular purpose, such as the German panzers, because the specialist techniques needed for the panzers, or atomic weaponry or other sophisticated expertise, cannot be controlled by any of the earlier management systems.

The Construction Industry faces the same problem but for the most part, because of its splintered structure and under capitalization, hasn't recognized the problem which is even further aggravated by the tendering processes. This is a far greater problem than can be solved by simplistic solutions such as undefined group working, or simple coding systems. The management structure must clearly be based on functional need and must allow the maximum flow of information. There are of course many possible ways of doing this, but one type of structure is proposed as a hypothesis.

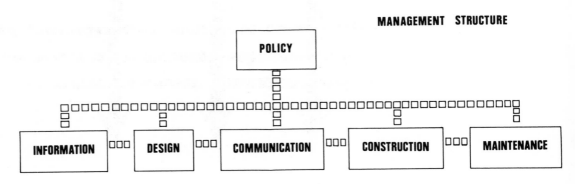

Figure 42

This functional organization not only represents the functions of design and construction as a total process, but also represents the information flow.

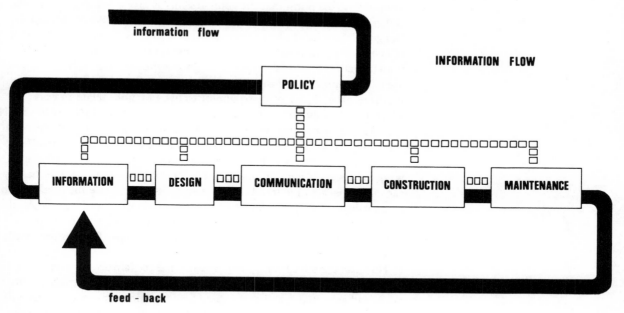

Figure 43

This is not a professionally-based organization, but a functional organization, and it is within this that the processes will be examined, not as a traditional situation nor a package deal, but purely as a way of getting a job done. After that, because it is modular, it can be augmented as one desires according to the need of the type of contractual system that seems to be desirable. It allows for the Contractor to be separated, as at present, or integrated as suggested. It can in fact be contained within one man if desired, as it relates to function and not to size.

POLICY can be established as a specialist group within the management team and created for particular tasks, or kept as a permanent part of the organization, but whichever it is, it is essential that the function of this group is clearly understood and recognized. Its work will be to evaluate the programme of work entering the system, to establish the background against which it will be carried out, and ensure that resources are available. This programme must also be monitored. In order to do these jobs properly, it is essential to have access to data of the right kind at the right time. If we are to make the most of available technology, it is fairly certain that the computer will play an increasing part in the system, and in this proposed organization the obvious place for it is in INFORMATION. However, as the range of data is infinite, INFORMATION must have direction as to the possible needs of the organization so that it can collect and store the most relevant data, and for this, POLICY must give direction.

Management in each of the other functions must equally be aware of this policy, and this raises the question of management throughout the organization. Management can operate in its traditional professional role,

127

or multi-disciplinary roles, or in the proposed functional system, and so it is necessary for these alternative systems to be compared.

In the professional office under the traditional system, it is so common to be almost the norm that the good designer is promoted to group leader and above, where he becomes an administrator and seldom designs again. Design talent is lost to management, because the pay is better and in order to keep him in the organization. Promotion is necessary even if his talent is no longer used, and furthermore, it ignores the fact that he has no management training. But if the situation is examined carefully, it can be seen that very often, many of these administrative functions relate to work which could easily be carried out by a properly-structured INFORMATION unit. Large practices recognizing this fact, increasingly employ office managers, but their efficiency is often restricted by the formation of the office.

The professionals who have a sound practical knowledge, but who are weak on design, often find that they have a poor career prospect. Generally, career prospects in the traditional system do not encourage the development of a particular talent or motivation, but rather, operate on the principle of promoting people who are good at a task into new work situations until they are ineffective, and at this point, promotion stops. This has been well-illustrated in the Peter Principle.

How can the education system be expected to train an Architect for instance, who must be fully competent in man's physiological needs, society's needs and aspirations, and at the same time be a first-class designer, as well as being competent in management and financial administration? He needs to be all of these things and more in theory, to be even a junior partner. This is only a short list of his necessary talents, in addition to which, he must be knowledgeable about all the Acts of Parliament, Regulations, and latest research relating to building. It may be a pleasant idea that the individual should be able to roam at will over all of these areas to give job satisfaction; but the risks are enormous. Surely there must be another way to give job satisfaction without running these risks. In any case, the public attitude to all of the professions is changing at an incredible speed, and failings are immediately called to account.

The breakdown into functions may be resisted by the traditional members of the team, but it is significant that much of the work that has been acclaimed in recent years, has been carried out in offices organized in similar ways to this functional grouping. If the functional type of organization is operated, a good designer can have a career structure right through to top management without having to keep changing his role. Similarly with the other functions, where members of the communication team for example, can specialize in the practical aspects of building without feeling inferior. If someone wishes to gain experience of the whole process, he can move from group to group and in this way cross-fertilize the organization, but otherwise a personal expertise will be developed. Furthermore, INFORMATION has now assumed a proper place in the organization.

This type of organization, allied to the proposed system, can eliminate a further problem which is caused by a confused flow of information.

In the traditional situation, decisions, which as we have seen tend to be put off to the last minute, are allowed to overlap to such an extent that items which should have been researched and evaluated at the briefing stage are still being found out at the working drawing stage. Examples have already been given in earlier chapters.

This muddled and inefficient system is often applauded, but in fact, is far from being professional in the sense of meaning a job well done. A truly professional way of working cannot possibly incorporate such confusion because it negates the whole basis of design, which is to integrate the known facts into a unified whole. This overlapping is not discouraged in present systems, because it gives an impression of speed and the failures of the system are corrected by those that make the mistakes. The only way the defects can come to light is when there is a substantial breakdown in the system. The impression of speed is of course completely false. When sketch plans are rushed through without consideration of the major issues, these unmade decisions are then moved down the process, sometimes waiting until construction has actually started, before being resolved. The longer the decision is delayed: the more factors there are for it to interact with, and the greater the effort, and the greater the time needed to resolve the problem. This way of working not only causes time and resources to be wasted, but causes senior professional staff to become involved in seeking information which is not their job. It also causes frustration between members of the team (Figure 44).

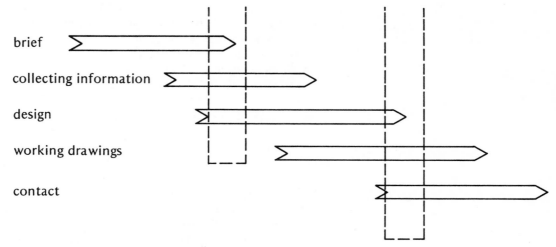

brief

collecting information

design

working drawings

contact

Figure 44

In the proposed management structure (Figure 42) each section completes its own part of the work which is clearly defined by its function, and the management of each section hands over a completed 'package' to the next section. This has the advantage of ensuring the state of each 'package' at the completion of each function. This dramatically reduces the interactive aspects of the process. It also places a responsibility upon the designer to complete his design in every respect before it is passed to COMMUNICATION, and this is now possible because:

(a) He has more time because administrative details have been removed and he has a better information source.

b) Design will contain all those disciplines relating to Design. Architects and Landscape Architects as designers. Quantity Surveyors as economic advisors, and Mechanical and Electrical Engineers as environmental consultants. Other design needs such as model-makers can also be included.

It might be argued that this type of organization will isolate the design team from the client/user because INFORMATION is collecting the brief and CONSTRUCTION is building the job. The true situation is that INFORMATION gathers together the major parts of the designer's background information, allowing time for a direct interaction with the user and, because of the system, it is now possible for a proper dialogue to take place. As for the other end of the process, the design team must still be responsible for the consequences of their design decisions but not necessarily involved in their administration on a day-to-day basis.

The initial client contact must be through POLICY, which allocates resources and alerts INFORMATION. As the satisfaction of the client's needs will depend upon the quantity and quality of resources, it is necessary for POLICY to ensure that these are made available to each section at the right time, and then monitor the progress. To do this manually, for even a moderate size organization, is a long and laborious task. Given a sufficient bank of historic data, it is possible to forecast, within fairly close limits, the type and quantity of resources required, not only for any individual project, but for a programme of work. It is also possible to monitor the projects. But whilst there are many offices with sophisticated systems, there are many with no means of carrying out the task at all.

In the proposed system, it is possible to use the MpAMPI resource allocation program described earlier, and this can operate as follows. The same Manpower files as those in the MpAMPI process are used, only the types in this case represent the category of professional and technical resource, and their particular expertise. This is to enable the machine to select, unless otherwise instructed, the person best matched for the job. At the same time a normal office checklist is related to a network in which the significant stages which particularly affect progress are highlighted. This can, for example, enable one hundred and twenty activities to be monitored from little more than a dozen specific inputs. In setting up the program, each project is fed into the machine with its appropriate target dates and with an input of resources available. Any deficiencies or surpluses are highlighted. It is a matter of office policy whether start dates or end dates are used, but it is recommended that end dates are chosen because this in the end is the most significant date. By the checking of only, say, fifteen points over the whole process, the progress of a project from start to finish can be monitored. If the programming of both design and construction are integrated as they can now be, even with a Contractor in a competitive situation, the whole resource allocation program can be operated against the completion date of the project. This means that the design can be developed in an interactive fashion with client/user involvement, whilst at the same time being aware of programmed completion dates. As many of the parts of the process will be handled by the computer, it can itself monitor these stages without causing frustration and annoyance to staff, as in the usual checking systems. If the agreed programme for a project is related to the computer diary program, the input of, say, a structural layout can itself be checked against this programme. Output of progress will again be personalized according to the level of information required. POLICY for example, will not want to know if the programme is being maintained — it will only want to know if anything goes wrong. Unnecessary documentation can be avoided by getting the machine to produce the names of only those jobs which are failing. If further information is required, this will be given on the print-outs for each function at the appropriate management level who are provided with a description of the failure. Finally a print-out for the person responsible for the delay which will give him full details of the problem. Alterations in the programme, either for individual projects or for the whole programme, can be carried out quickly and simply by the machine. The computer has often been criticized for producing a vast amount of useless information, but this is always a product of bad computer management. A good system will provide only that information which is necessary, and no more. In fact it should be used to sift and purify data so that only the minimum hard data has to be handled. By the same token, complaints of the cost of updating in any part of the system are often due to poor construction of the computer system.

This system of monitoring work can be pursued still further and will be dealt with in the last chapter, but even at the level just described, the effect of the organizational change, together with the provision of improved tools, could have a very significant effect upon efficiency which will reflect itself in better rewards, and better status and conditions for those in the team. The objective must be to produce a positive attitude to the solving of problems, with a consequent reduction in the backlog which inhibits new work, because problems are largely solved when the objective is clearly decided and defined. Achievement then becomes a comparatively simple matter.

POLICY is in a position to review the situation, and this will now be done before the whole process is brought together as a working machine in the next chapter, and before a scenario for the future is discussed in the last chapter.

It would be naive to think that the introduction of a computer with new processes will create an El Dorado. The real problem is that as life is like a swiftly flowing river, one has to swim very hard to stay in the same place and even harder to make a little progress. Unfortunately, a short relaxation means that one is swept backwards very quickly. It is the same with communication. If our ancestors had said that it was no use striving for improvement because the gains would only be small, if any, we would certainly have slipped backwards to an impossible degree, even perhaps to extinction, because other factors such as birth rates, which affect scale, have changed the world and its problems.

At present, there seems to be more concern over competition for the position of project manager, than trying to get the process right. The proposals that have been made may not be the best by any means, but the significant fact is that *every program that has been described exists somewhere;* and once they are brought together, by whatever persons or organization, they will present a formidable competition for the present traditional systems, for a whole variety of reasons.

131

It is probably as well to recount the factors which can make such a system incapable of being ignored.

1. The design and pre-contract processes can, if necessary, be achieved in days, if not hours.
2. The evaluation of the design must be of a high standard thereby reducing the risks of failures.
3. Client/user can participate in the design process.
4. A whole variety of different contractual methods can be employed.
    (a) The system can provide blank Bills of Quantities for pricing by Contractors in the traditional fashion. (A longer process).
    (b) The system can be used with serial tendering processes as recommended in government publications.
    (c) The MpAMPI + P system, with or without computer processing, can be used to give the maximum advantages described.
    (d) Design and Construct contracts or 'package deals' can be accommodated if thought to be advantageous.

It may be argued that Planning Approvals and other administrative procedures will slow down the process and therefore make the changes not worthwhile, but in the first place these procedures do not apply everywhere in the world; and in the second, it may be that if the process can be seen to be related to the common good because of increased participation, some inroads into these most restrictive regulations might be made. In fact, many of the present formalities could easily be dispensed with by using computers. Checks by local authorities to ensure that requirements are carried out are often long and laborious but could be checked quickly with existing digitizing equipment using compatible systems.

User participation has been referred to many times, but the balances between designer and user are particularly delicate and a lot more study is necessary before any real understanding can be achieved, but social trends in this direction are unlikely to change.

A variety of contractual options have been listed above, but whichever one is selected, the basic requirements remain the same.

1. A co-ordinated data bank of information.
2. Continuous and uninterrupted information flow.
3. Modularity enabling different contractual arrangements to be employed.
4. A system orientated towards the total problem rather than individual processes.

At first sight, the processes suggested in this book may appear to favour only the large organizations, but it is clear from the many different possible methods of operating the system which have been described, that even individuals can operate such a system and that the only thing necessary is a desire to improve the information flow. In fact such systems, making the best use of computers using generalized systems, is more likely to preserve the integrity of the design team than any other system. In 1968 the Author said in a lecture on computer aided design at the Royal Institute of British Architects:

> 'If, as a profession, we were to grasp the nettle now, I believe that the Architect could, and should, return to the position he was in in by-gone ages, where he was able to have immediate access to specialist information already partly synthesized and allowing him to spend the majority of his time in creating the final forms with which he wishes to express the aesthetic and functional needs of the society in which he lives.'

Since that date, there has been little or no progress in this direction in the Construction Industry whilst during the same period the development of integrated computer systems improving and speeding up the flow of information in other industries has proceeded with incredible pace, giving the users greater flexibility rather than less.

As can be foreseen, the tide of events will not be stopped because we are afraid of change, because, like water, society's demands find their own level, if necessary by taking another course. This has happened by systems being developed which try to speed up the process but which at the same time reduce the design team's choices.

In January 1976 the R.I.B.A. journal published the following glossary to explain the types of systems in use for obtaining contracts in the housing sector only. There are of course many others for the non-housing sector.

GLOSSARY

Package deals. There is no architect between client and contractor. Bids on the brief are invited from contractors and they prepare the design.

'Develop and construct' (PSA/DOE). The architect prepares a detailed site layout and selects dwelling types from a range of PSA standard plans based on metric house shells. The selected contractors tender on the basis of the layout and plans; a performance brief, and specification clauses, their own method of construction and foundation drawings; and preliminaries and bills of quantities for external and site development works.

The successful contractor then "develops", i.e. details the design into final working drawings to suit his own method of construction and finally carries out the construction. All drawings produced by the contractor have to receive the architect's approval before use, but nonetheless the contractor bears liability for any defects which appear within six years of completion of the works and which result from a deficiency in design. Special clauses are used in the building contract to define this liability. Unlike the GLC's procedure (see below) the work does not have to receive local authority approval.

The Develop and Construct Programmer and Guide prepared by the PSA describes the process and can be obtained from the Regional Housing and Planning Office.

'Design and build' (NBA). The architect prepares a site layout using metric shells and selects contractors with ranges of dwelling plans to fit the metric shells. The contractors tender on the basis of the layout and their own plans; a performance brief and specification clauses as required

by the local authority; their own system drawings and typical foundation drawings; and preliminaries and bills of quantities for external and site development works.

Develop and construct (GLC). The client appoints the architect who then prepares layout, plans and elevations. Several contractors tender, using any system they may have. The selected contractor produces the working drawings, specifications, bills of quantity for the building contract. If the GLC architect approves this work, the contractor chooses his own sub contractors. (If not, he resigns.)

Common plan range (Scottish Local Authorities Consortium): a range of diagrammatic metric house plans illustrating optimum arrangements of accommodation complying with the Scottish Housing Handbook standards and the Scottish Building Standards Regulations. The range covers variations of frontage, depth, aspects, and family size and enables house types to be selected which make the best use of sites without pre-empting the designer's choice of building method, form or treatment.

Library of standard details (SSHA). The Scottish Special Housing Association has developed the principle of the Common Plan range to produce a range of house plans capable of realisation by three alternative building methods (brickwork or blockwork, No-Fines concrete, and timber-frame). The SSHA range is prepared as a library of house plans from which house types are selected for individual layout situations. The Association has commissioned Edinburgh CAAD Studies to develop computer applications providing a graphic display of each house type in the SSHA range, permitting amendment and updating of plans, and linked to a print-out of contract drawings and bills of quantity.

Figure 45

133

The interesting thing to note is not only how far many of them restrict the contribution of the design team and how little they do to bring the industry into a completely integrated system, but how much of the gross building output has been lost to the design teams. In some cases, the designer becomes a cipher to be disposed of in the first economy cuts, and yet even these solutions would appear to be preferable to the professions rather than creating a unified design and construct team with closer integration with the community.

The development of systems to short cut the traditional processes to save time and money must continually put the traditional system and the valuable expertise of its exponents at risk.

Chapter 9
THE MACHINE

Before examining a possible integrated system, it is necessary to consider the reasons why there has been so little involvement by the industry, and in particular, the professions in the use of computers.

As is well known, computers were originally developed as electronic calculating machines, and so it was natural that their main use and development was originally directed towards financial systems. Inevitably, many of these systems were badly conceived and/or badly operated, and this gave rise to all the stories and jokes and criticisms which were eagerly told in order to reinforce already established resistance. In spite of the criticisms and failures, computing, particularly in the financial field, has grown until it touches our lives at almost every point, most of the time without even being realized. Better and speedier service which we seek and demand in other fields is often supplied, unobtrusively, by computer systems. But, in spite of this development, the building industry and the professions have largely ignored the whole area in spite of considerable encouragement in the form of large numbers of lectures and conferences. The main exceptions are very few. There are private, local Government and Government offices using computers in comparatively limited areas such as Bills of Quantities, and there are also a few large contracting organizations mainly using them for accounting systems. The major exceptions have been well publicized. There appears to be a number of reasons why this lack of acceptance has happened.

1. Architects, by the nature of the task are the initiators of the design process, but on the whole are not numerically inclined. Whilst they concentrate on the creative design aspects, they prefer to leave measurement and calculation to other professions; which is perfectly reasonable in normal circumstances as no man can do everything. But in this area, his disinterest has been more than unfortunate. Even in the cases where the architect has believed in the need for computing, he has invariably either delegated the task to an allied profession such as the Quantity Surveyor, or to a young enthusiastic Architect, neither of whom has the power to change the overall system. The Quantity Surveyor is usually prevented from making any changes which might affect the traditional design process, and therefore his area of operation is restricted to the point where it is extremely difficult to make a system economically viable. This has been seen in the deve-

lopment of computerized Bills of Quantity. The young enthusiastic Architect is also restricted, not only in his own area of operation, but also in knowing what the total system is all about. He is invariably restricted, as is the computer systems analyst, to examining the processes already going on, and this leads to the 'mechanization of the horse' syndrome.

2. Early successes in some aspects of computer-aided design split the professions into those against (the majority) and those (the few) who thought the whole problem was simple and could be solved in a matter of months. Some years later, the enthusiasts are generally agreed that it is a longer process, and at the heart of the problem lies the problem of handling large quantitities of data. Those original unfounded expectations have now been overtaken by the steady sound work of those remaining in the field, but unfortunately, those who were against the whole idea only see their original views confirmed by the failures.

3. As the original development of computers was for accounting systems, many computers came under the control of accountants, and in Local Government, under the control of treasurers, which had, at the least, a psychological effect.

4. The fragmentation of the industry meant that there was no agreement on the information flow, which was also accompanied by low capital investment at a time when computers were expensive. Now that prices of computers have dropped, the interest has waned.

5. Competition between the professions for the position of project leader, or leader of the team, added to the traditional separation of design and construction, has made it difficult for anyone to co-ordinate the whole process. Because of the size of the industry, the international computer manufacturers appear to have been willing to invest large sums of money to develop systems for the industry, but they have found it impossible to pick up any thread in this tangled skein because the quantity of data in this building industry is vast and unstructured, and the processes confused.

Assuming that it is desirable to work towards a computer-aided solution, there are a number of factors to be considered in the purchase and development of computer systems. Firstly, there is the question of equipment. There have been two major developments in recent years which have greatly changed this situation. It is now possible to carry out work on inexpensive mini computers, which a few years ago could have only been done on very large and expensive computers.

Furthermore, the price of computers related to their power has dropped dramatically in a short space of time, and will probably continue to do so. These developments make it possible for comparatively small offices to buy and use their own equipment. It is often felt that even at these reduced costs, firms are unable to support such equipment, which may be true, but depending upon the office formation and its work, it can be viable even in very small offices. The combined fees of all the professions involved for medium and large projects represent a substantial sum of money, and individually are needed and justified but, as suggested in this book, a lot of this cost is absorbed in abortive labours and bad communication. If offices were to group together, not within their own professions but functionally in order to form an integrated process, then they could not only financially support sophisticated systems, but retain their own identity within a faster process. It could also provide the opportunity for small offices to obtain the benefits of large offices, without some of the disadvantages.

There is the alternative of using bureau services which in some applications has advantages. Because there are continuous changes in the law, regulations and so on, computer programs, even when perfected, cannot be left without maintenance. For example, when taxation laws change, the machine must be instructed to take account of them. Just as we ourselves have to be re-programmed, so does the machine, even though this might be a minor modification to the program. A bureau has the advantage of specializing in a field and thereby, updating the processes for a whole range of clients which is invariably cheaper than doing it individually. The type of work where bureaux may be considered is for batch processing and similar processes, where answers and print-outs are only required in hours, rather than seconds. Just as an evaluation of the response time needs is required when making a choice between bureaux and house systems, the same applies to the choice of equipment and processes when 'in house' systems are developed. It is very nice to have instant answers to everything, but if it only means that the information is left unused for a long time, it could mean that unnecessarily expensive equipment is being used. On the other hand, there are some instances where the designer, who may wait a long time for answers in the traditional methods, becomes irritable if he has to wait 30 seconds for an answer from a computer.

As it is the data which lies at the heart of computing in a practical environment it means that a lot of work can be done before even purchasing a computer. If realistic looking plastic inflatable models of computers were to be placed in every office, the effect in itself would be astonishing. Even the idea of using computers makes an organization question the way it operates, and this in itself invariably means a reduction of abortive processes. Once an office becomes orientated towards the use of computers, data and processes are gradually rethought, but if this is allowed to develop fragmentally, the same problems occur as those we have seen in the whole traditional industry. An inter-disciplinary team (POLICY), giving leadership and direction, and ensuring proper co-ordination can begin to regularize the process even by using simple techniques such as edge punch cards which cost very little. Each saving in resource goes towards the research on the next saving on resource, and this builds up until the equipment can be bought. When this moment arrives, a decision has to be made on whether it should be purchased or hired.

Hiring arrangements, as previously stated, usually work on the basis of the capital cost divided by four or five years. After this period, the rental reduces to a very low figure. This is of course only a very rough guide, but is sufficient to illustrate the problem that a machine on hire for more than five years will cost more than buying one outright, but, there is the advantage that during that period, when new and better machines are being brought out quite frequently, the hiring system does enable an office to keep up to date more economically.

It appears that sometimes when resources are expended on computer aids, a lot of the resources go on members of the design team writing programs rather than on analysing the system. Generally, it is much more efficient and economic, and a higher level of competence obtained when the design team analyse the job to be done, and let those who are specialists in the field put it into operation. Ideally, there should be the POLICY team co-ordinating the analysis of the process, which is then translated by an industry-orientated systems analyst who understands the industry jargon and process, but who can also instruct conventional system analysts and programmers. This team should be constantly aware of future needs which must be continuously evaluated.

Anyone who has been involved in interdisciplinary team exercises, such as the courses run at the Institute of Advanced Architectural Studies at York, will know the incredible number of decisions that can be made on a project during a weekend course. The outstanding success of these courses depends upon the short response times brought about by bringing all the design team together. This in effect, is similar to parts of the system proposed, which uses computers for the same purpose. Apart from the speeding up of the information flow, what they have in common is invigoration followed by fatigue. Any computer process must take into account the fact that many of the processes, because of their increased speed, can cause excessive concentration for over-long periods. The problem is not making people work in this way, but having to stop them. Just as in playing chess, or any other game where one's concentration is completely held, the users of computers can, in some areas, become so involved in their work that they fatigue themselves.

A further aspect of the introduction of computer techniques is the way in which these are put into general office operation and this can be of considerable importance. One thing is certain, that when any change is introduced, whether this is for good or bad, progressive or retrogressive, it will not satisfy everybody as there is some inherent conservatism in us all. This means that where an integrated system has to be developed, care must be taken to ensure that the system is brought into operation in the best possible manner, and this must, to a large extent, depend upon time, and the type of organization. There may be some useful points to consider here. One is, that if traditional systems are left around at the same time as new systems are introduced, people will on the whole, drift back to the ways with which they are most familiar. This has led to some people operating a procedure which ensures that all traces of the old system are removed, leaving only the new system for use. This is particularly important with documentation. The second point is, that it is almost impossible to convert a whole office at a single stroke. It is probably desirable to bring together a team of the most progressive people in the office, who will represent the whole process, and who can operate a miniature of the whole system. When this is working, they can return to their original places in the organization to consolidate the implementation of the process, and act as disciples of the new processes.

The following diagrammatic description of the whole process is mainly based on work carried out with the County Council of West Sussex, the London Borough of Hackney, and at the University of Reading, and is, for the most part, a commercially operational system. Work carried out in allied areas, at other Universities, Polytechnics, and offices added to the system would make it possible to produce a whole process in a 'black box'. This would be on the basis of a major processing centre for the major processes, and installing mini-computers in offices which would carry out all the necessary local processing, only referring to the major computer for the more complex operations or batch processing.

There is the very real possiblity that an organization could by-pass the professions and the traditional industry, and provide a service with which it would be difficult to compete in terms of cost, speed and basic performance. Even the present state of knowledge and experience can produce systems for this type of situation.

A building system, linked to a library of parts with full MpAMPI back-up, and kept up to date with terminals anywhere in the country, would enable clients to walk into an office, participate in the design of their own buildings, and have tender costs and full evaluation within a few hours, with production drawings as soon as Local Authority approvals had been obtained. The scale of the operation would be dependent upon the complexity of the building system, and this is why so much space has been devoted to this aspect.

It is against this background of speed and service that the present professions may have to operate, in addition to those other standard systems already in operation. Alternatively, they have the opportunity of providing the same service with all of those additional advantages of professional experience that they alone can give, and with the freedom of design which they have been used to, if the process is rationalized. The last chapter will try to offer suggestions as to which way the future may develop.

Already, work by the Ministry of Agriculture, Fisheries and Food Development Advisory Services and The Scottish Farm Buildings Investigation Unit have progressed a long way along this route for farm building. This work is for the improvement of environmental conditions for animals.

The following description is intended to bring together into one cohesive whole, all of the processes which have been described in this book, but it is not intended to be a description of a particular system. Any office or organization wishing to develop a system may wish to use this as a framework of discussion or for agreement on the scope of their own proposal and its relationship to the whole. It is also to be hoped that the industry, professions, and Government, develop similar holistic systems which can provide design flexibility with speed, economy and improved performance evaluation, and retain the talents and knowledge of the existing professions.

The Process

The following description indicates the type of data which might be stored and the ways in which it could be used in a computer-aided information system. There will also be supplementary comments to assist an appreciation of the relationship of parts, and also to suggest where certain types of computer programs may be used in the process.

Data

Before anything can be processed, by whatever means, there must be a bank of data which will be discussed before considering its processing.

Files on Man (including women and children!)

Whilst the data is all about various aspects of man, the files will be used for different purposes, namely:

(i) Briefing and predesign
(ii) Pricing

The first aspect is one which can grow over the course of time, and which will relate the physical requirements of human beings to age and sex.

Age	Sex	a	b	c	d	e
1	m f					
2	m f					
3	m f					
4	m f					
5	m f					
⋮						
102						

Figure 46

The sort of data which will be inserted into columns a, b, c, etc., will be, for example, the range of the desirable air temperature needs of human beings and all the other significant factors in the development of a true brief such as the sound emission range of human beings, and their acceptable receptive levels of sound and range. These, together with man's physical attributes, are put into age ranges because clearly, there are different standards at different ages.

The data is that which is needed to ensure that the physical environment will match the human need. The following diagram from the report of the Scottish Farm Building's Investigation Unit may illustrate the point, even though it is for pigs!

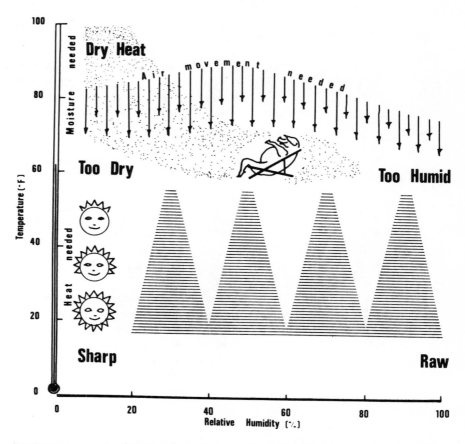

SCHEMATIC DIAGRAM OF BIOCLIMATIC INDEX FOR GROWING / FINISHING PIGS

Figure 47

The other aspect of man which needs to be kept on file is his salary or wage rate, and as in any conventional accounting system it must be capable of being grouped into categories, for example:

(i)   The MpAMPI need for trades.
(ii) The classification for resource allocation at pre- and post- tender stages.

The basic needs of the first are:

Ref	Manpower Type (By trade or specialism)	Price Date	Unit Measure	Basic Rate per hour	Gross Rate per man
	"	"	"	"	"
	"	"	"	"	"
	"	"	"	"	"

The reasons for these breakdowns are as follows. Manpower type is to enable the reference of any particular trade to be related to the appropriate building activity Mp x A = Labour rate. The price date is important so that anyone using the file will know to which date the manpower rate relates. The conversion of a weekly and hourly rate to a minute rate is necessary because of its association with an activity time. There may be in the order of 100 types for building generally, and 150 types for each of the mechanical and electrical trades.

The basic needs of the second is:

Ref	Manpower Type (by profession, specialism, trade etc.)	Category	Name (if required)	Availability

The reference column is the equivalent of a code. The manpower types are needed for the allocation of resources to the correct area of work, and the category is to denote the particular specialisms of anyone named in the next column. It is of course not necessary to name and categorize these if this is not required. Availability must be kept up to date to prevent resources being used which are already expended.

Activity Files

Activity files will be accessed for three purposes:

(i)   Briefing and pre-design
(ii) Construction
(iii) Resourcing

In the first instance these would be different sections and aspects of the same file because of the need to retain rapport within the industry on item (ii), but gradually this could become one homogenous file.

The needs of each of these categories will be as follows:

(i)   *Briefing and pre-design*

Ref	Activity	Compatibility

(ii) *Construction*

Ref	Activity	Time (in minutes)

In the first instance, these construction activities may be, for example, transportation of concrete by barrow and hoist, where the concrete is in the materials file, and the barrow and the hoist are in the plant file. Later, these can be simplified to become the same type of activities as proposed in earlier chapters for briefing and pre-design.

(iii) *Resourcing.* This can and should be the same as (i) but must be particularized and coded as the activities are to be resourced.

All categories will include the basic activities of man such as walking: walking with various loads; walking upstairs with or without loads; standing and working at horizontal surfaces; stacking; and so on; as well as more specialized activities such as, prepare planning application, for the resource file.

Materials File

It is suggested that the materials should be filed on a matrix basis, as already described, based on the CIB master lists. These include the Master list for materials, Master list of components, and the Master list of building elements including prefabricated units, however constructed. If the range of work so requires, there are two further lists which may be used: Master list of buildings and the Master list of services.

It may be found convenient in the early stages of setting up a system to have a conventional file for pricing as follows:

Ref	Description (Conventional)	Price	Price Date	Source of Price

Plant Files

These will be the contractor's records of plant to be used, plus a facility for price records.

Ref	Description	Price Date	Source	Price

Equipment Files

Ref	Description	Price Date	Source	Price

Location Files

This is merely a reference file using the twelve digit National Grid system for identifying a space upon the earth to a level, if required, of one metre. This degree of accuracy of identification will of course not always be necessary, but the important factor here is that the system is rather like a series of gradually reducing sieves, making it possible to use a grid at any level, and thereby use any of the spatial dimensions as a container of information. For example, if one were to count beetles at the metre level, and inset the information into the files, the beetle population could be counted over any area at any higher level of grid. These containers can also be useful for planning records as well as for the meteorological file. Therefore this system provides identification of a location and also contains information related to it.

Meteorological File

As the required degree of building enclosure comes from the meteorological environment of a given location, it is necessary for these to be recorded. Some examples of meteorological information which are important to buildings are as follows:

Temperature range	●	For degree of insulation and thermal storage
Wind forces	●	For structural stability
Rainfall	●	For watershed

These are only a few examples of the sort of information which should be instantly available for any area where a building is to be designed. These files become particularly important when designing systems such as solar energy and wind-power systems.

Files Generally

There are many files which will be built up according to need which may include some of the following:

1. Building regulations and codes
2. Landscape data
3. Payroll

The files that have been explained are only those which are basic to the fundamental process described and not meant to be exclusive. Once a data bank has been started on rational lines, it tends to grow quite naturally and quickly. All of the foregoing files can be set up within an office, but could more desirably be set up regionally or nationally for the benefit of all. The following files will be tailored to the needs of the individual, office or organization:

Dimensional Rules. Most people work to some dimensionally co-ordinated system. The best of traditional work is carefully related to brick dimensions, whilst many industrialized systems relate to varying metric grid systems. If a co-ordinated library is to be prepared, it is necessary to establish the dimensional basis upon which this library will be built. These can, dependent upon the type of organization, be incorporated into an office design guide which can indicate the framework within which the library can be used.

Catalogue. When most building components are selected, they are selected from a catalogue and not the shop drawings. In the same way, a catalogue of the standard drawings in the library can be prepared. This catalogue must particularly indicate reference and options. If further information is needed by the designer, he can easily go to the Assembly drawings, described next, by using a related reference or code.

Assembly Drawings. These are fully detailed construction drawings which are automatically called up by using the Catalogue reference, and are also related by code to the Specification. The assembly drawings are orientated entirely towards the needs of the Constructor, and do not necessarily cover the same area as the blob description alone.

Blob Rules. The blob rules relate to the dimensional system decided upon, and also the type of work to which they relate. The blobs are extremely fluid in content, and therefore the rules must describe length, area, cube, or even concept, ensuring that they do not overlap each other. The essential fact of a blob rule is that it codifies an aspect of building for both drawing and measurement. Once the rule of measurement for any particular zone or function is decided upon, it is easy for any option within that functional zone to be measured and still retain its identity and compatibility.

Blobs. These are the actual measurements which are made in accordance with the blob rules of any material, component, or part of a building, and its environs. e.g. any type of partition can be measured against the blob rules for that item. This will mean that they can be compared under such headings as MpAMPI, sould resistance, weight, stability, etc. because they have all been measured on the same basis.

Specification. Either a National Building Specification, or organization or office specification can be related to all parts of the system, thereby reducing the need for repeating information, and at the same time making updating and corrections easy.

Schedule of Works. Within categories of work such as housing, schools, factories, etc., there is a limited number of building activities. Therefore, if a programme of building work allows, the preparation of a unit schedule can facilitate the process. A list of all the building items such as those found in a typical Bill of Quantities is made on a unit basis for the activities expected in this building programme. Whilst it is desirable to make it as comprehensive as possible, it does not have to be complete because this list is related to the MpAMPI files already described, and therefore other scheduled items can be manufactured endlessly from those files. This in effect provides the following:

Ref   Traditional Standard Method of Measurement descriptions consisting of Mp x A + M + PI = TOTAL, can be rationalised and translated into a file schedule as follows. Profit is not included because this is a percentage to be applied to the whole.

145

Ref	Description	Price Date or Amendment Date	Price

This schedule will be automatically updated whenever each of the MpAMPI files is updated. Clearly this happens at regular intervals in a controlled manner. As this now provides an up to date price list of S.M.M. items, tenders may be invited for the profit or management percentage to be added to these rates. It may be argued that tenderers would need to apply different percentages to different parts of these rates, but this is not the case because of the reasons already given in earlier chapters. A global percentage approach is satisfactory because much of the risk element has been removed.

Tender Enquiry Schedule. This must include those significant factors which will affect the contractor's management and which are not included in the schedule, such as:

Size of contract and number of storeys
Location
Type of construction
Start or completion date of contract
Special restrictions such as noise restrictions etc.

This document, together with the updated priced schedule, enables a tender percentage to be obtained. When this percentage is added to the prices in the Schedule, the design team are then in possession of a set of tender rates for the work to be carried out. All pricing will now be as a contract figure.

When the design is completed, and if required, a priced Bill of Quantities can be produced automatically by the computer upon which a formal contract can be based with a total tender figure.

Network. A file of standard network stages is needed against which the MpAMPI and other criteria can be allocated by the machine. When these individual stages are put together by the Constructor they can be processed for resource allocation.

Times Used. It is useful to have a times used program in a real world environment to prevent a continuous build up of data without anything being thrown away, as tends to happen on manual systems. The computer is able to keep a record of the number of times any item is used. This record can be reviewed by POLICY from time to time and the justification of storage considered.

Error Print-Outs. All systems must include such a program in the system as it is one of the great advantages of using computers. Mistakes which might be overlooked by human operators can, if the programs are properly written, be thrown up for questioning.

Diary. This is a simple entry of dates for an unlimited period, with an opportunity for referencing, and is a computer version of a conventional 'bring

146

forward' manual system. It can be linked to a number of processing programs as already suggested.

Now that the data bank has begun to be assembled, the process can be examined. This is not a particularly difficult problem, but it is difficult to illustrate in two dimensional book format. All that will be shown therefore will be the main process, with reference only to sub-problem solving programs. The program descriptions are deliberately generalized to enable a search to be made in books such as Computer Program Description for Architects, published by The Department of the Environment, or Hutton and Rostron's Computer Programs for tne Building Industry 1974. Programs (encircled numbers) are available somewhere for every sub-problem referred to, with the exception of the analysis of Building Regulations.

Key to programs referred to in figure 48

1. Resource allocation program
2. Diary program
3. Basic site computation program
4. Building regulations program
5. Digital plotting program
6. Location/meteorological search program
7. Activity sortation program
8. 'Bubble' diagram program
9. MpAMPl update and print-out program
10. Analysis of functional criteria program
11. General suite of interactive programs (see Appendix)
12. Evaluation programs
13. Matrix search program
14. Environmental evaluation program
15. Normal line printing and plotting programs operating on data already input (see Appendix)
16. Co-ordinated structural programs
17. Mechanical and Electrical engineering programs (see Appendix)
18. Analysis of symbols in MpAMPl functional criteria program
19. Analysis and sortation programs
20. Resource allocation program
21. Validity programs
22. Normal records file related to matrix materials and components file
23. Cost in use evaluation program
24. Grid referencing program
25. Matrix search program
26. Resource and management program

CLIENT/USER

POLICY

INFORMATION
(including computer processing)

DESIGN

① ② ③④ ⑤⑥ ⑦

EXAMINE

A) IF BUILDING REQUIRED
B) IF NEW BUILDING REQUIRED
C) RESOURCES REQUIRED AND AVAILABLE
D) TIMESCALE
E) POLICY FOR PROJECT

CLIENT/USER INPUT

AGREEMENT OBTAINED

INPUT DECISIONS ON ABOVE

ALLOCATE PROJECT TO DESIGN TEAM

EXAMINE OFFICE RESOURCE NETWORK AND
PRODUCE PRELIMINARY PROGRAMME AND
ENTER INTO DIARY PROGRAM

OBTAIN SITE DETAILS
COLLECT RELEVANT REGULATIONS, CODES, ETC.
PREPARE FOR DESIGN NEEDS
PROCESS SITE DETAILS
ACTIVATE LOCATION / METEOROLOGICAL SEARCH
AND COMPATIBILITY PROGRAM

PROCESS AND PRODUCE SORTATIONS

INTERACTION WITH CLIENT USER TO DEVELOP
BRIEF AND PROGRAMME

DATA ON ACTIVITIES, LOCATION AND SITE
OBTAINED FROM INFORMATION

INPUT NUMBER OF PEOPLE AND THEIR ACTIVITIES

COMPUTER SORTATIONS EXAMINED AND VARIOUS
PERMUTATIONS EXPLORED IN TRADITIONAL MANNER
AGAINST BACKGROUND OF FUNCTIONAL REQUIREMENTS
OF LOCATION

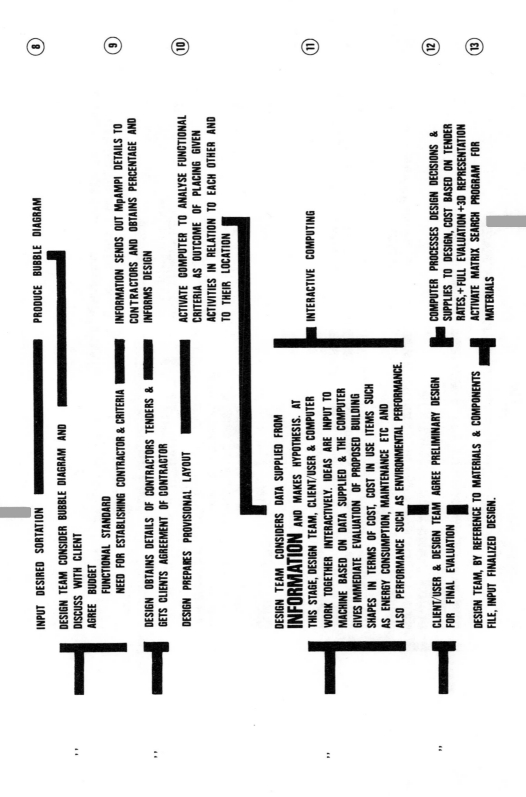

Figure 48

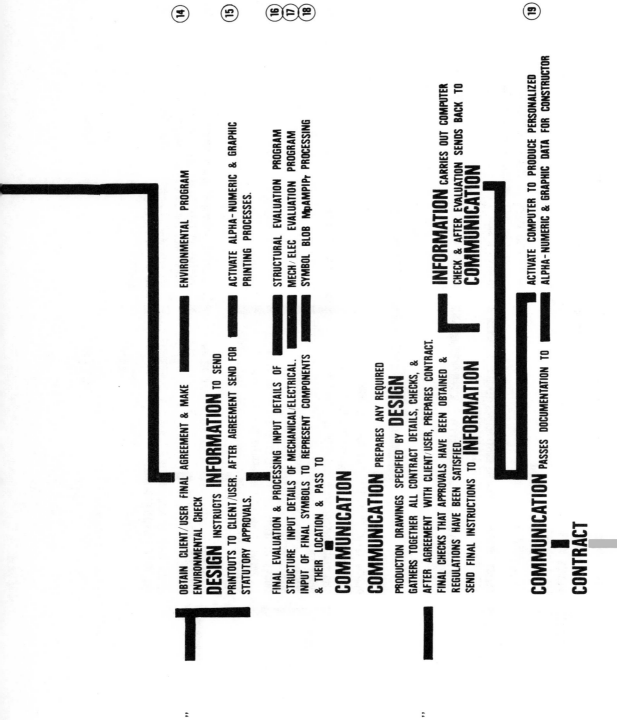

⑭ OBTAIN CLIENT/USER FINAL AGREEMENT & MAKE ENVIRONMENTAL CHECK

DESIGN INSTRUCTS INFORMATION TO SEND ENVIRONMENTAL PROGRAM PRINTOUTS TO CLIENT/USER. AFTER AGREEMENT SEND FOR STATUTORY APPROVALS.

ACTIVATE ALPHA-NUMERIC & GRAPHIC PRINTING PROCESSES.

⑮ FINAL EVALUATION & PROCESSING INPUT DETAILS OF STRUCTURE INPUT DETAILS OF MECHANICAL/ELECTRICAL. INPUT OF FINAL SYMBOLS TO REPRESENT COMPONENTS & THEIR LOCATION & PASS TO

STRUCTURAL EVALUATION PROGRAM
MECH/ELEC EVALUATION PROGRAM
SYMBOL BLOB MpAMPIPr PROCESSING

COMMUNICATION

⑯⑰⑱ COMMUNICATION PREPARES ANY REQUIRED PRODUCTION DRAWINGS SPECIFIED BY DESIGN GATHERS TOGETHER ALL CONTRACT DETAILS, CHECKS, & AFTER AGREEMENT WITH CLIENT/USER, PREPARES CONTRACT. FINAL CHECKS THAT APPROVALS HAVE BEEN OBTAINED & REGULATIONS HAVE BEEN SATISFIED. SEND FINAL INSTRUCTIONS TO INFORMATION

INFORMATION CARRIES OUT COMPUTER CHECK & AFTER EVALUATION SENDS BACK TO COMMUNICATION

⑲ COMMUNICATION PASSES DOCUMENTATION TO CONTRACT

ACTIVATE COMPUTER TO PRODUCE PERSONALIZED ALPHA-NUMERIC & GRAPHIC DATA FOR CONSTRUCTOR

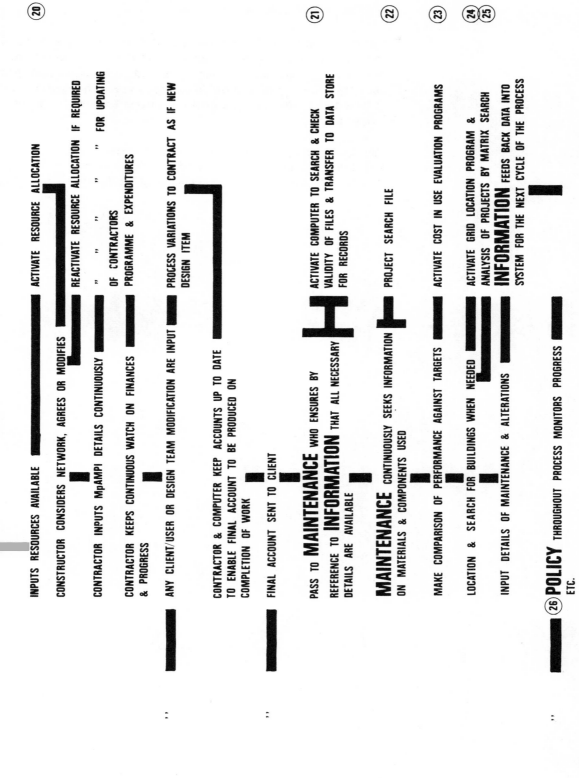

(20)

INPUTS RESOURCES AVAILABLE ■■■■ ACTIVATE RESOURCE ALLOCATION

CONSTRUCTOR CONSIDERS NETWORK, AGREES OR MODIFIES ■■■■ REACTIVATE RESOURCE ALLOCATION IF REQUIRED

CONTRACTOR INPUTS MpAMPI DETAILS CONTINUOUSLY ■■■■ " " " " FOR UPDATING OF CONTRACTORS

CONTRACTOR KEEPS CONTINUOUS WATCH ON FINANCES & PROGRESS ■■■■ PROGRAMME & EXPENDITURES

ANY CLIENT/USER OR DESIGN TEAM MODIFICATION ARE INPUT ■■■■ PROCESS VARIATIONS TO CONTRACT AS IF NEW DESIGN ITEM

CONTRACTOR & COMPUTER KEEP ACCOUNTS UP TO DATE TO ENABLE FINAL ACCOUNT TO BE PRODUCED ON COMPLETION OF WORK

FINAL ACCOUNT SENT TO CLIENT

(21)

PASS TO **MAINTENANCE** WHO ENSURES BY REFERENCE TO **INFORMATION** THAT ALL NECESSARY DETAILS ARE AVAILABLE ■■■■ ACTIVATE COMPUTER TO SEARCH & CHECK VALIDITY OF FILES & TRANSFER TO DATA STORE FOR RECORDS

(22)

MAINTENANCE CONTINUOUSLY SEEKS INFORMATION ON MATERIALS & COMPONENTS USED ■■■■ PROJECT SEARCH FILE

(23)

MAKE COMPARISON OF PERFORMANCE AGAINST TARGETS ■■■■ ACTIVATE COST IN USE EVALUATION PROGRAMS

(24)
(25)

LOCATION & SEARCH FOR BUILDINGS WHEN NEEDED ■■■■ ACTIVATE GRID LOCATION PROGRAM & ANALYSIS OF PROJECTS BY MATRIX SEARCH

INPUT DETAILS OF MAINTENANCE & ALTERATIONS ■■■■ **INFORMATION** FEEDS BACK DATA INTO SYSTEM FOR THE NEXT CYCLE OF THE PROCESS

(26) **POLICY** THROUGHOUT PROCESS MONITORS PROGRESS ETC.

Figure 48 continued

151

The effect of such a system is to provide:

(a) Reduction of time between client demand and commencement of work on site, due not only to new information methods and the use of new equipment, but also the tendering process with its associated administration being carried out in parallel with the design process. The report by Slough Estates Ltd. (1976) shows the disastrous effect of making the two processes sequential.

(b) User/Client participation in the design process.
(c) Integrated information flow throughout the system.
(d) Greater opportunity for an evaluation of the design.

Chapter 10
THE FUTURE

Looking into the future is not only traumatic, but forecasts are so very often wrong. Kahn & Wiener (1967) who probably have more of a reputation than anybody for looking into the future, have said:

> 'Unfortunately, the uncertainties in any study looking more than five or ten years ahead are usually so great that the simple chain of prediction, policy change and new prediction is very tenuous indeed.'

They continue:

> '. . . . at the minimum, such studies, even if only partially successful, contribute to interesting lectures, provocative teaching and stimulating conversation, all of which can broaden horizons and increase creativity.'

It is obvious that a post-war forecast of energy for the U.K. would not have taken into account the North Sea oil or gas, but that is not to say that looking at the energy problem didn't stimulate its investigation.

When putting up buildings which are costly to replace or reorganize, or giving consideration to the needs of education, it would be improvident not to think of the future. Today's students will, it must be assumed, be working in the industry up to forty years from now, and today's building designs will probably be in use for a lot longer than that. For these reasons alone, it is impossible to ignore the possible social environment for building and its design and construction for at least twenty years ahead.

There are many techniques for forecasting, some of which use computers, and these techniques, apart from the well known individual poll or committee system, include Delphic, Digitometer, Trend extrapolation, Substitution Analysis, Cellular analogy, Acceleration analogy and Scenarios, to name but a few. If the response times for design could be reduced, it might become possible for some of these techniques to be used for the creation of environments for society to grow into, rather than as too often at present, growing out of, because we are reacting too late. This could provide a new dynamic responsive environment.

The question must arise as to whether there are stable trends upon which the future can be forecast. If there are, they would probably include:

1. The growing appreciation of the equality of men and women throughout the world is unlikely to be reversed.
2. The increase in the world-wide dissemination of information is unlikely to stop.
3. Because of both of these points, the demand for an equalization of the share of the world's resources is unlikely to reduce.
4. Similarly, a demand by the mass populations of the world for a standard resembling those of the 'rich' countries is likely to increase.
5. The trend towards the abolition of boring and and repetitive mental work will continue just as physical labour has been enormously diminished by the effects of the Industrial Revolution

It would not be unreasonable to assume from this, that new processes must be devised to meet a future world demand. The professions have already come under a pressure that would have never been thought possible thirty years ago, and there are many signs that the next thirty years will bring even further pressure for productivity and change upon them. The contracting part of the industry at the multi-national level has recognized this and has been adapting to new circumstances, but for the most part the smaller contractors have changed little, perhaps because they are restricted by the amount of adaptation to the process that the designers are prepared to make.

There are many arguments made against change in the future. The first is that the present tendency towards a low level of building activity in the western world will tend to discourage innovation and change, and encourage a reversion to traditional techniques. There are two aspects of this argument. One is the assumption that a low level of building activity will continue. Just as people in boom periods think it will go on forever; so do people in recession. Few people have ever forecast with any accuracy either a boom or a slump. The other aspect of the statement is the implication that recession stops innovation and change. History shows that the reverse is true. To take one example alone, the slump of the 1930's in the United Kingdom brought greater changes to the Construction Industry than had been seen for a long time before or since. Recession gradually encourages the natural instincts of man to adapt and survive.

There are clearly a lot of people dissatisfied with their present working and living conditions, and whilst this exists, ways will be sought to solve this need. Self-help and self-build is only one of the new attitudes which has already emerged to fill this void, and there will no doubt be a lot more, but before these possibilities are examined, it is necessary to bring together the proposals made so far.

A number of proposals have been made, many of which have had to range, not only from the very general to the very detailed, but have been interactive between design and information methods. This has been because the degree of standardization, or non-standardization we expect in the design of buildings affects the quantity of data, and the processes we use. The fluctuation between the general and the particular is due to the fact that the problem is an extremely large and complex one, and in which there are detailed factors which have a large effect on the whole system. Whilst a great deal more could have been described in detail it may have destroyed the overall concept.

To summarize briefly these proposals:

1. Changes in our philosophy increasingly change attitudes from a belief in an absolutism proposed by a few, to a belief that each individual has the right to self-expression.
2. The effect of this individuality is to use standardization and production to transfer manual and physical mundane tasks to machines, thereby giving a greater opportunity and more time for personal expression.
3. Systems can be developed which enable these machine productions to become available quickly and easily to a user, who is able to satisfy his personal and individual needs with the help of the design team using new methods.
4. There is the alternative that the same systems can be used on a purely commercial basis, probably limiting individual involvement, but representing formidable competition to the traditional process because of the considerable savings in time.

Clearly there will not be one simple answer to future building. The range will obviously stretch from the traditional design processes, using traditional construction and information methods, to completely integrated computer-aided design and construction systems. The question for the future will be what share of building programmes will be devoted to each, and whether new processes will be developed.

In making predictions, it is fairly certain that the major aspect of future change is undoubtedly going to be an increased demand for speed, which has already expressed itself in the new forms of design and construct systems. These can emasculate the traditional design teams processes to the point where they can largely be dispensed with for a large part of the major building programme. The percentage of the U.K. national building programme which is handled by systems such as those listed in the R.I.B.A. glossary is already very substantial. It is possible that this has come about, and will continue to increase, because of resistance to change and a belief that tradition gives individuality, which ultimately leaves the design team with less freedom than if they had worked collectively to develop new systems.

Apart from this factor of speed, demanded by the 'have nots' who are no longer prepared to wait, there is also a growing concern by the student about his right to enforce his views upon other members of society; and society's doubts about whether he should in any case do so. This has expressed itself on the one hand in the development of housing systems such as PSSHAK and so on, and on the other hand by demands for user participation. Both of these create considerable problems unless technology is brought in to help. It is one thing to experiment with user participation in single storey buildings on limited and isolated sites, but how can complex buildings in urban environments be carried out in this way without using new technology to test and evaluate?

In the beginning of this book it was shown that each individual must be unique, because he is building up his own unique data bank from birth. It must therefore be right that he should have the opportunity for personal expression even if this has to be within a framework of fashion or style. Neither the existing design procedures nor construction systems permit this need for individual expression to be possible. Any buildings, or groups of buildings tend to be standardized by the design team in order that it has rationality. But this means that flats, for example, in any single block or blocks are standardized, even though the users have different and individual tastes and needs. Apart from those occasions where the user is the client, individualism is only able to express itself in places such as Soho, and the souks of Marrakech, and similar places in every country in the world, where individual expression has overcome the disciplined dictums of the bureaucracy and the idealized built environment of a designer, who almost certainly does not live or work in that environment. It is interesting that these areas of individual expression, which may on the one hand be called, by some, visual slums, are on the other hand extremely popular. If we move, in the future, towards this type of environment to suit the present views of the individual in society, we shall need the best technology for evaluating each changing demand against Building Regulations alone, for it is certain that these will not go away.

Another significant factor in considering change will be the general attitude of society to life in general. Renaissance beliefs in finiteness and absolutes have gradually been eroded. These create an atmosphere of living for today and not building or planting for tomorrow which may create a need, not only for speedier design systems, but faster building systems, or even disposable systems. In all this, the industry and the professions will have to become more capital intensive, and work together as a team. Small might be beautiful, but it will only become possible with the use of large technologically based background systems and here may lie the clue. The telephone is one of many examples of a personal tool giving the individual an undreamt of freedom and potential by using a very high level of technology which stays in the background, and which, by and large, is unobtrusive. If one thinks of its faults, one should also think of what would happen to present society without it, with all that that implies. Computer systems will be set up in the same way, and there is little doubt that they will, but the question remaining is whether they will be set up to provide for freedom and change, or will they be harsh, unchanging, and inflexible systems?

The real area for concern is in the structure of the data, and not in the machines and programs. As discussed in the early part of the book, every piece of data can be interpreted in a variety of different ways, and this gives a flexibility of thought which is necessary to the democratic processes. On the other hand it is possible, as has happened in some totalitarian regimes, for the information to be always slanted in one direction, and it is in this that the danger of data co-ordination and computer systems lie. it is possible to produce computer systems which can grow and change and adapt to human needs, and provide most of the needs of client users and the industry as a whole, but will it happen, or will alternatives happen first? In the United States of America, more than six million people already live in mobile units. In the United Kingdom there is an ever growing demand for rapid and economic solutions which is being met by the use of mobile units, and which can be seen multiplying at an astonishing rate: are they already by-passing the system? Will this industry expand and develop to the point where traditional processes are only used for exceptional buildings? The use of computers in other industries has brought a service to vast numbers of people which until recently could only be given to a few. Might the same not happen in building?

But in order to make a transition to a more capital intensive industry to achieve this, there must be a steady building programme which will only come about by the industry gaining strength by working together as an integrated industry, and avoiding its present fragmentation. In this way it would be in a better position to create a demand for its services, if not to create its own demand.

All of the processes described in this book have been on the basis of a tool for use by the industry; just as tee squares and calculating machines are tools. None of the proposals suggest that the decisions of the human being should be transferred to the machine; rather the reverse. But there are those who fear that the computer will design our whole environment without our intervention, but by definition, this largely implies that the machine would be a replica of the brain and there are few who would believe this to be even possible, let alone near at hand. Therefore, for the forseeable future, we are only having to face the problems of supplementing our minds, in the same way as we have already largely overcome the problem of supplementing our muscles.

Another factor which may create significant changes in the future is the increased use of mini computers and the implementation of computer terminal systems. The development of larger organizations such as the growth of Local Authority architects departments, etc., has come about largely because of the problems of communication. In the early part of the century the core of such organizations were small, and work of whatever nature was handed out to individual practitioners. As the speed of change increased, the problem of updating and instructing a large number of disparate firms became more difficult. By bringing these services together, the lines of communication could be reduced and the response times maintained. This has further led to the inclusion of more and more professions and specialisms within an ever growing organization. But with the sort of processes proposed in this book, the trend can be reversed because the data bank is common to all who need it, via terminals. This trend is likely to happen in all industries with the effect that increasingly people will be able to work at their own convenience and in their own home, only coming together for necessary personal interaction. In Architecture and building this could be of considerable importance because it would enable the whole design team to work and live within, and contribute to, a community. In this way technology can be used to bring us back to that which was so valuable in earlier community life. The techniques for this are already being implemented through the present television systems. All this is apart from the impact of very cheap micro-mini-computers which will probably be available in the next few years. All of this might provide the new impetus which is needed to give direction to Architects and the public alike, who have returned nostalgically to the conservation of existing buildings as a reaction to the post-war spate of buildings with which they are so disillusioned. Clearly, we must return to a positive approach to new building.

Technology is often reviled as it is said that mass production causes pollution and reduces choice; but these sort of statement are far too bland. Even a cursory view of lower technology societies show their pollution levels are often high and their choice pathetically small. Only slowly are the potentials of mass production beginning to be exploited for the benefit of personal expression.

Toffler (1970) says:

'The finding that pre-automation technology permits diversity is borne out by even a casual look at . . . the supermarket . . . the array of goods they offer the consumer is incomparably more diverse than any corner shop could afford to stock.'

Individualism in clothes is an outcome of cheap mass produced products, but in Architecture, there are still only a few signs of these new changes being expressed.

Erskine's Byker Wall in Newcastle-upon-Tyne is an example of user participation within a predetermined structure. The primary school at Eastergate, Sussex, previously referred to, was designed as a backcloth for human activity, and not a dominant piece of architecture in itself, in the same way that John Cage's composition '4'33"' was a frame into which outside noises could enter as full collaborators. As it is now technologically possible for computers to be used to help this approach, because they can inform local communities and users of the availability and performance of components, they may in the future expect to play a greater part in the design of their own environments, using the design and construction team as a sort of midwife to help them express their own desires.

Basic information banks, using the simple co-ordination proposals suggested, could be held by local authorities on their own computers, and the information could be supplied for example through their library services to the design teams, in the same way as one obtains information through books. Alternatively, they could be set up commercially, or by voluntary consortia. In these situations, communities will be able to develop their own environments where architecture will only play a supporting role to human activity. It will undoubtedly be said that the whole idea is either too simplistic, or too complex. But incredibly complex systems, such as the telephone system, have grown at a very great speed from very simple principles.

It may be that the professions will wait until commercial enterprise brings together all the programs mentioned in this book and puts them into a simple 'black box' computer system. In such a situation, the client/user will be able to see his needs developed, evaluated, and priced within hours, and if the building systems are economic, what will happen then?

The Construction Industry of the future will undoubtedly have room for both of these proposals as well as the traditional system, but if either new system is developed, it will bring considerable pressure to bear on existing information methods.

LIST OF APPENDIXES

I. Description by I.B.M. United Kingdom Ltd. of a suite of computer programs developed by West Sussex County Council.

II. A selection of graphic outputs illustrating the W.S.C.C. (1971) System.

III. Description of the graphics module used in a production environment by West Sussex County Council, and now used by the Department of Construction Management, University of Reading.

IV. Description of computer runs for a contract system used in a production environment by West Sussex County Council, and now used by the Department of Construction Management, University of Reading.

Appendix I

The following report was prepared by I.B.M. United Kingdom Ltd. as a description of a computer system developed in the County Architects Department of West Sussex County Council.

It is included, not only as one example of the implementation of some of the processes described in the book, but to show that even in 1971 it was possible to operate such systems in a necessarily financially viable environment.

The building system

System Features

This document describes the features of the Building System, conceived by West Sussex County Council.

Some details are given about each of the sections of the System and also of the collection of files referred to as the data base.

The final details and the sequence and method of implementation may change, depending upon the requirements of those parties involved in the implementation.

April 1971

1. Introduction

1.1 The Building System consists of a number of programs which enable its users to retrieve and pass on information in terms which they can each understand, rather than in a form dictated by other users.

1.2 There is a collection of files, referred to as the data base, which contain permanent information on materials and units, on shapes (for graphic design and production drawings) and on activities (for network calculation and resource allocation).

1.3 The programs can be divided into five sections:

    1.3.1 enquiries into the materials file and selection of items for communication of the building design;

    1.3.2 communicating design details to the system, using a visual display unit with a light pen;

1.3.3   contract documentation, including bills of quantities and production drawings;

1.3.4   project control, where resources can be allocated over the activities needed for the administration of the construction;

1.3.5   feedback, including creation of files, recovery and reorganization, and updating with new information.

2. *The Data Base*

2.1   The logical relationship between the principal permanent files of the data base is shown in the appendix.

2.2   There are three paths to the Materials file: functional, plain language and where-used.

2.3   In the functional path, the files are used by the terminal conversation program firstly to develop, by question and answer, a profile key showing the performance which the user requires. These questions are held for each functional group in the Function data set. Secondly, the conversation program reads from the Function Group data set, a block of all the performance keys of materials in that functional group the keys are scanned for the best matches to the profile. The blocks are pointed to form the function data set and contain the minimum of information so that the scan can be as fast as possible.

2.4   In the plain language path, the technique adopted is the same as for the functional path. The main difference is that here the conversation program develops a description of the required item by means of a noun and qualifying adjectives.

2.5   Any item within the materials file may have various component materials and each record contains pointers to its components. For the purpose of updating, a Where-Used file shows all the items of which each material is a component.

2.6   The Materials and Where-Used files both have variable length records because of the need to hold a variable number of pointers and a variable amount of descriptive information. To ease the problem of embedded spare space for modifications, a conceptual DISAM organization is used.

2.7   For each of these two files, an index is held in record identifier sequence (ISAM organization). This index has embedded spare space so that keys can be kept in sequence as much as possible and minimum use is made of independent overflow areas. The data files themselves are BDAM organization and are in sequence after each reorganization, but any additional records are added at the end of the file. This means that there is no shuffling of variable length data and less wasted space; also that the system is less sensitive to unevenly distributed insertions. The records are blocked to fixed length blocks of 3000 bytes, and this gives the block address of the block containing the record required.

2.8   The Symbol file holds information about the relative co-ordinates of the shapes that can be used for the graphic design section. The co-ordinates are relative to some pre-defined origin which, when the shape is placed on the design grid, will correspond to the grid point that was detected upon with the light pen. The organization is BDAM and the records are retrieved using a pointer contained in the Materials file. A maximum of 20 lines are contained in each record.

2.9 The project control section contains programs to manipulate critical-path-type networks and to perform resource allocation over the network. There are logical breakpoints in most networks of construction projects and between each breakpoint is a sub-net made up of the activities required to complete a given part of the project. These sub-nets are pre-defined and can be 'added' according to certain rules to form a complete network. The Networks file holds these sub-nets and the items to which they relate.

3. Enquiries Section

3.1 This is a teleprocessing service which allows a user at a terminal to enquire into the Materials file, and to select materials for later use in the design section.

3.2 It is intended to use TCAM under OS/360 and the IBM 2740 Typewriter and IBM 2260 Visual Display Units.

3.3 The user may specify his requirements either by functional characteristics, by plain language or by the actual user code of a material, after having identified himself to the System by his own or his department's identification code, to ensure that he is entitled to receive the information he seeks. These specifications are made by means of a conversational program where the enquirer is asked a series of questions and has, for each question, a range of possible answers from which to select.

3.4 Except where the enquirer specifies the user code of a material, the conversation will have the general form illustrated in the appendix. After the identification check, the enquirer signifies the type of enquiry and is then asked to select the group of interest (level, category and sub-category).

3.5 A more detailed description is then established by the user answering up to 8 questions. The details may be in terms of performance required (functional) or of descriptive adjectives (plain language).

3.6 The enquirer has the opportunity to change any of his answers and to give relative importance to each of the answers.

3.7 The system then searches the complete group of interest for a number of items most nearly matching the enquirer's specification. A brief description is returned of these items, together with an indication of how well each one meets the enquirer's specification. Optionally, the enquirer can ask for further details of any item and he can select out any item for later use in the graphic design section.

3.8 Several conversations can be in progress at once, the number of conversations depending upon the amount of core storage available to the conversation program.

4. The Design Section

4.1 Having selected the materials and items that he wishes to include in his building, the user is able, in this section, to communicate the design of his building to the system. This is done in a symbolic manner, where 2-dimensional plan shapes represent 3 – D parts of the building. Each shape communicated to the system is said to be filled with one of the material assemblies selected in the enquiries section. The allowable shapes for each assembly and the amounts of materials needed to fill the shape are extracted from the data base and passed to this section via the Job file.

4.2 The position of each shape and its filler material are indicated by means of a grid on the IBM 2250 Graphic Display Unit. As a picture is built up, a digital form of it is held in core and later transferred to auxiliary storage so that each picture can be re-generated as necessary. A number of pictures will be necessary to represent a complete job and as they are completed they are related to surrounding pictures so that their context is always known.

4.3 The architect's estimate of the cost of unit measure of each material is taken from the data base via the Job file and as the design is communicated to the system, a cost check can be made under several sub-headings and in total.

4.4 When the total design is finished and is acceptable to the designer, the total quantities of each material and assembly are known and any rogue item (not represented by shapes) can be entered via cards. Enough information is now available to the system for expanding the requirements of each material and item, in preparation for producing bills of quantities and production drawings.

4.5 At the display unit, the designer makes his choices and positions the shapes by pointing the light pen at the screen and pressing a switch to cause a 'detection'. The system first displays a list of the functional groups and the designer selects the one with which he wishes to start. A list of the items available in this group is then displayed and when one is selected, the shapes which this material item can assume are shown. The lists of items with each group and the shapes which each can assume, could be larger than there is space on the screen, so forward and backward paging is provided. Symbols for positioning and rotating shapes are also on the screen, and by detecting on a shape symbol, a positioning symbol and a grid point, the system draws the shape in the required position. This is repeated until a whole picture is built up; it can be saved by pressing a key on the programmed function keyboard attached to the Display Unit.

5. *Contract Documentation*

5.1 The documentation referred to in this section includes bills of quantities (listed by sub-contractor if being sent out in open tender or priced if in a serial tendering situation) and production drawings, drawn on a plotter.

5.2 Since there are already in existence several suites of programs which produce this documentation, it is not intended to write any more. This section will, therefore, consist of interface programs to allow such suites to follow on with the output from the previous graphic design section.

5.3 The principal tasks of an interface program are:

    5.3.1 the conversion or manipulation of the material identifier code.

    5.3.2 the reading of the data base for more data, including details of component items.

    5.3.3 the accessing of other data sets, possibly unique to a particular user, for further information.

6. Project Control

6.1 Network analysis can be applied to the actual construction of the building (of interest to contractors) or to the administrative tasks that precede and succeed the construction (more useful to local authorities and private architects). However, the programs in this section may be applied to either problem, the difference being in the input data.

6.2 For many types of building and parts of buildings, the administrative activities involved are always the same in content and sequence, and the durations and resources will vary with the quantities of materials, ie the size and quantity of the buildings. Hence, a file can be maintained of standard sub-nets for these activities; these are on the Networks file of the data base and are related to the items on the Materials file itself.

6.3 The programs in this section will manipulate critical path networks and will allocate resources over the activities and produce relevant reports to indicate the results of the processing.

7. File Maintenance and Recovery

7.1 The usefulness of the System depends largely on the accuracy of the information contained in the Data Base files. Since there are several interrelated data sets in the data base, they must all be kept at the same update level, and the user must be able to recover any file or part of a file if a correction occurs.

7.2 There are programs to create records for the Materials file from existing WSCC files which contain units, items, PC components and materials. The Where-Used files are created directly from the Materials file and the same programs can be used for recovery. The Function and Function Group data sets can be created either totally from card input data or by creating 'skeleton' data sets from the Materials file and then updating these at a later date.

7.3 Modifications to the data base files are done in 'batch' mode, ie not while on-line for enquiry terminals and display units. An edit program will ensure that all relevant data has been submitted in the correct format and the update program will update all the appropriate files at once, saving the original records for recovery purposes.

7.4 Programs to reorganize, dump and restore files are provided and also a program to list the principal files in a suitably edited and readable format.

Appendix II

A selection of graphic outputs illustrating the W.S.C.C. (1971) system.

The placing of a 'light pen' against the answer selected automatically brings up the next question or process. Similarly lines, symbols, etc. are inserted by the same 'light pen'.

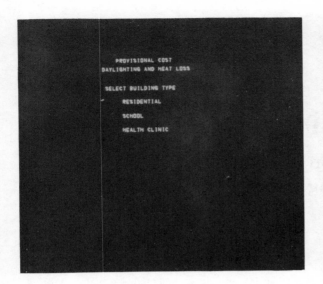

1 User selects building type

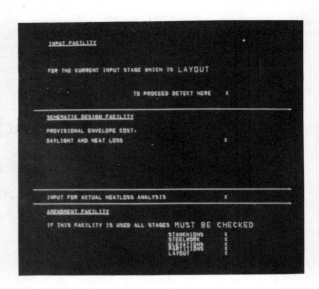

2 User chooses type of facility he wishes to use

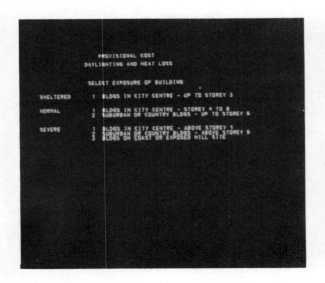

3 User selects exposure conditions

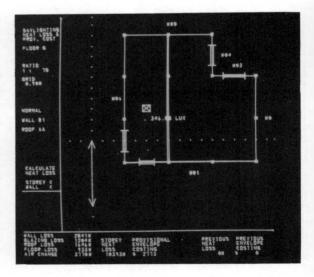

4 User 'draws' sketch plan and then tests for such things as estimated cost, heat loss, air changes, lighting levels, etc.

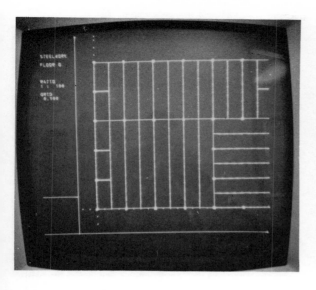

5 When a satisfactory design has been agreed, structural system is developed

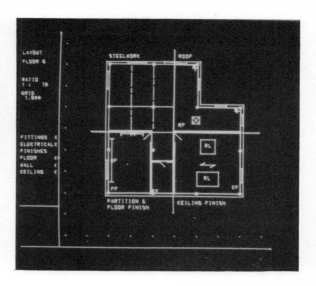

6 Each quarter of this picture illustrates:
    Top left — insert structure
    Top right — insert roof
    Bottom right — insert ceiling
    Bottom left — spacedividers and finishes

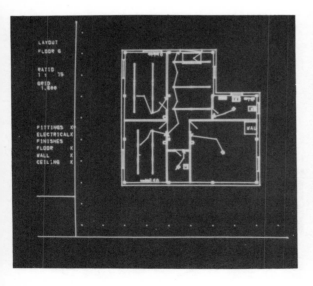

7 User inserts mechanical and electrical engineering services

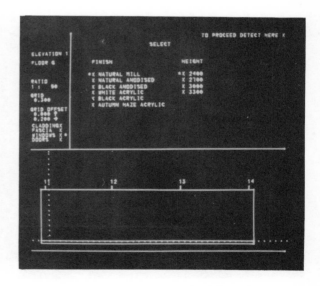

8 Computer offers choice of materials for window selection, together with elevation

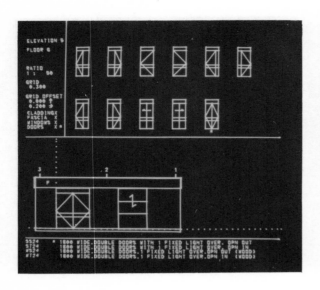

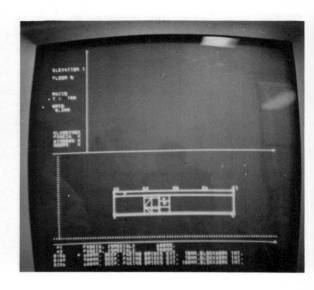

9　When material has been selected, computer offers those windows held in store which are suitable for the project. User selects and indicates position. Computer automatically 'draws' window.

10　User can 'scale up' or 'scale down' at any time

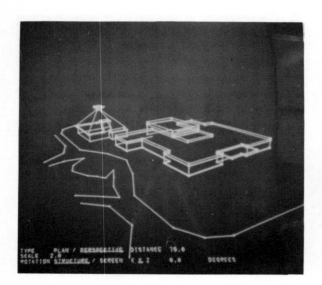

11　User can select perspective routine at any stage. The degree of detail depends upon the input already supplied to computer

12　Digital plotter output can be quickly coloured to provide realistic presentation

Appendix III

Description of the graphics module used in a production environment by West Sussex County Council, and now used by the Department of Construction Management, University of Reading.

```
┌─────────────────────────────────────────────────┐
│       WEST SUSSEX ARCHITECT'S COMPUTER SYSTEM     │
│                 GRAPHICS MODULE                   │
├─────────────────────────────────────────────────┤
```

This Module of the West Sussex Architect's Computer System uses a Visual Display Unit with Light Pen assembly to provide the facility of communicating design decisions to the system.

The program stores, on disk, records containing details of a) the graphic data sets used and their relationship one to another, and b) the units of quantities, with costs, used in each design solution specified by the designer. The information contained at b) can be transferred to magnetic tapes for use by a following module called 'Contract' module. The information contained at a) is accessed by a following module called 'Plotting' module. Upon request a summary of the costs of the building being displayed will be shown on the screen and a print-out of a detailed summary is then automatically provided.

This program does not require the intervention of a programmer at any time. Architectural technicians have been trained to operate the module in less than 8 hours.

FOR DETAILS OF FILES SEE PAGE 174 *et seq*

172

COMMUNICATION OF DESIGN DECISIONS USING THE VISUAL
DISPLAY UNIT

The program is being used in a multi-programming environment and
occupies the 2nd priority partition of an I.B.M. configuration which
uses a model 360/40 (256K) operating under Operating System release
18.

The size of the partition used is 76K
The peripherals used are I.B.M. 2250 (V.D.U.)
                           I.B.M. 2311 (Disk Drive)
                           I.B.M. 2400 (Magnetic tape Drive)
                           I.B.M. 2540 (Card Reader)
                           I.B.M. 1403 (Line Printer)

To call the program from disk a small deck of cards are used.
The work area of the 2250 screen is 10″ x 8″ representing 40′ x 32′.
The remaining area is used for displaying 'Menus' and Messages. A
floor plan can be described in an average time of 25 minutes. Roof
and Foundation plans can be described in an average of 10 minutes.
No elevations or sections are required or produced.

PRODUCTION OF MAGNETIC TAPE CONTAINING DETAILS OF
UNITS OF QUANTITIES USED IN EACH DESIGN SOLUTION.

To transfer details of design solutions used, to magnetic tape for
subsequent processing requires approximately 60 2400 (magnetic
tape drive) to the configuration.

**WEST SUSSEX ARCHITECT'S COMPUTER SYSTEM
GRAPHICS MODULE**

MESSAGE FILE – Contains a list of Informative messages displayed
for the operator.

Size – 100 x 44 Byte records. Each record is 10 words, plus one
control word.

The file occupies three cylinders on a disk pack.

Input is from cards.

PICTURE FILE – Provides space for details of 60 work areas and
stores the names of the graphic data sets used and
their relative positions in the work area, together
with the names of the design solutions, associated
with the graphic data sets and their costs.

Size – 240 x 1600 byte records.
Four records one work area.

The file occupies 14 cylinders on a disk pack.

Input is from program.

DATA FILE – Contains names and costs of design solutions selected
for the project together with the names of the
associated graphic data set(s).

Size – 6534 – 16 Byte records.
Each record contains unit infill code,
representative character and cost.

The file requires 14 cylinders on a disk pack.

Input is from cards and requires 7.3 secs. of C.P.U. time to set up.

SYMBOL FILE — Contains names and x.y. co-ordinate values of graphic data sets. Each set can contain up to sixteen lines.

Size — 50 x 1584 Byte records.

The file requires 12 cylinders on a disk pack.

Input is from cards.

WEST SUSSEX ARCHITECT COMPUTER SYSTEM
PLOTTING MODULE

The size of the partition used is 88K and the peripherals used are

I.B.M. 2250 (V.D.U.)
I.B.M. 2311 (Disk)
I.B.M. 2400 (Magnetic tape drive)
I.B.M. 2540 (Card reader)
Calcomp 750 (Magnetic tape drive)
Calcomp 663 (30″ Drum plotter)

Time required for transferring
graphic data set details from   Approximately 60 seconds for
disk to magnetic tape   each work area.

A grid to give scale to the drawings and a title block is plotted to A1 overall size immediately before the details of the plans. The time required for this is approximately 17 minutes. Average time required to produce the plans is approximately 10 minutes.

WEST SUSSEX ARCHITECT COMPUTER SYSTEM – CONTRACT MODULE

This module contains a suite of programs which accepts and manipulates sets of measurements to produce optional sortations of schedules of quantities in traditional Bills of Quantity items or schedules of Materials, Activities, Manpower and Plant.

Measurements are accepted by the program from cards or magnetic tape.

The program is being used in a multi-programming environment and occupies the 2nd priority partition of an I.B.M. configuration which uses a model 360/40 (256K) operating under Operating System release 18.

FOR DETAILS OF FILE SEE PAGE 178 *et seq*

VALIDATION – This program validates input and produces a) list of errors b) initial abstracts.

The size of the partition used is 46K

The peripherals used are I.B.M. 2540 (Card Reader)
I.B.M. 1403 (Line Printer)
I.B.M. 2400 (Tape Deck)
I.B.M. 2314 (Multiple Disk)

The processing time is 40 minutes.

The C.P.U. time used is 250 seconds approximately.

CORRECTION OF INVALID STATEMENTS

Correction of original input by Quantity Surveyors using cards.

VALIDATION. ABSTRACTS. BILLS OF QUANTITY. SCHEDULES.

This program validates input and produces a) List of errors (if remaining) b) Bills of Quantities in Trades (priced or unpriced) c) schedules of components for Advanced Information Schedules d) abstracts (with error messages).

The size of the partition used is 80K

The peripherals used are I.B.M. 2540 (Card Reader)
I.B.M. 1403 (Line Printer)
I.B.M. 2400 (Tape Deck)
I.B.M. 2314 (Multiple Disk)
I.B.M. 2311 (Disk Unit)

The processing time is 50 minutes approximately

The C.P.U. time used is 850 seconds approximately.

UPDATING LIBRARIES — These programs create or delete complete or parts of records held on existing libraries.

The partition size, used is 46K
The peripherals used are I.B.M. 2540 (Card Reader)
I.B.M. 1403 (Line printer)
I.B.M. 2400 (Tape Deck)

The processing time is an average 5 minutes.

The C.P.U. time is an average of 30 seconds.

ABSTRACT. BILLS OF QUANTITY (PRICED OR UNPRICED)

This program produces Bills of Quantities in Network Stages (Priced or unpriced). Abstracts in Network Stages.

The partition size used is 80K

The peripherals used are I.B.M. 2540 (Card Reader)
I.B.M. 1403 (Line Printer)
I.B.M. 2400 (Tape Deck)
I.B.M. 2314 (Multiple Disk)
I.B.M. 2311 (Disk Unit)

The processing time is an average of 80 minutes.

The C.P.U. time is an average of 1100 seconds.

OPTIONS — It is possible to obtain optionally, Bills of Quantities in a) Functional Groups, b) Work Sections (both priced and unpriced) c) sub-networks to networks together with Abstracts and error messages

The partition size used is 80K

The peripherals used are I.B.M. 2540 (Card Reader)
I.B.M. 1403 (Line Printer)
I.B.M. 2400 (Tape Deck)
I.B.M. 2314 (Multiple Disk)
I.B.M. 2311 (Disk Unit)

The processing time is an average of 80 minutes.

The C.P.U. time is an average of 620 seconds.

FILE OF ITEMS — This file contains approximately 6,000 measured items of work recording a) Name of item b) Description.

The size of the partition used is 46K
The number of records is optional
The processing time is approx. 120 seconds.
The storage device is magnetic tape
The file creation time is approx 63 mins. for 6,000 items

FILE OF QUANTITIES — This file contains approx. 2,600 units of measured items of work recording a) Name of unit b) Description c) Names of items of work included in unit, plus quantity and network stages.

The partition size used is 46K
The number of records is optional
The processing time is approximately 60 seconds.
The storage device is magnetic tape.
The file creation time is approximately 4 minutes.
Input is from cards.

FILE OF RATES — This file contains the prices to be applied to the measured items of work and records a) Name of item of work b) Rate to be applied c) identity of rate source. d) MAMP detail

The partition size used is 46K
The number of records is 5,000
The processing time is approximately 90 seconds.
The storage device is magnetic tape.
The file creation time is approximately 5 minutes.
Input is from cards.

FILE OF P.C. COMPONENTS — This file contains a list of approx. 4,700 components to be supplied or supplied and fixed by suppliers or Sub-contractors and records a) Name of component b) Description of component c) Name of supplier of component. d) Rates of each component with date when recorded

The partition size used is 46K
The number of records is optional
The processing time is approximately 120 seconds.
The storage device is disk.
The file creation time is approximately 8 minutes.
Input is from cards.

FILE OF P.C. COMPONENT — This file contains a list of the names
SUPPLIERS   and addresses of the suppliers of
                               components and records a) Name of
                               supplier b) Address of supplier c) Name
                               of component.

The size of the partition used is 46K
The number of records is optional
The processing time is approximately 1 minute.
The storage device is disk
The file creation time is approximately 20 seconds.
Input is from cards.

CONTROL BILLS — This file contains a list of approx. 2,500 items
                 of work in Bill of Quantity format used for the
                 evaluation of serial tenders in Trades or Net-
                 work sortation.

The size of the partition used is 46K
The number of records is optional.
The processing time is approximately 4 minutes.
The storage device is magnetic tape.
The file creation time is approximately 40 seconds.
Input is from cards.

MATERIALS — This file contains a list of approx. 2,000 materials,
            recording a) Name b) Description c) Unit of measure
            d) Rate to be applied

The size of the partition used is 46K
The number of records is optional.
The processing time is approximately 4 minutes.
The storage device is disk
The file creation time is approximately 40 seconds.

ACTIVITY — This file will contain a list of approx. activities recording a) Name b) Description c) Name of Alternative resource types able to perform activity. d) Time required to perform activity by c)

TO BE CREATED

FILE OF MANPOWER TYPES — This file contains a list of approx. 200 resource (man) types recording a) Name b) Description c) Rate to be applied

The size of the partition used is 46K
The number of records is 200
The processing time is approximately 1 minute.
The storage device is disk
The file creation time is approximately 15 seconds.

FILE OF PLANT TYPES — This file will contain a list of approx. resource (Plant) types recording a) Name b) Description c) Cost on site d) First cost.

TO BE CREATED.

Appendix IV

Description of computer runs for a contract system used in a production environment by West Sussex County Council and now used by the Department of Construction Management, University of Reading.

contract system STAGE 1

SET UP LIBRARIES

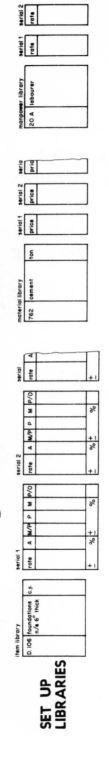

FILE CREATION RUNS

1.2. item library, priced or unpriced
3.4. materials library, priced or unpriced
5.6. manpower library, priced or unpriced
7.8. plant library, priced or unpriced
9.10. p.c. component library, priced or unpriced
11. p.c. suppliers library
12. control bill of quantities library
13. critical path network stage library

14a). unit quantity library-summary print
14b). unit quantity library-edited print
14c). unit quantity library-full item print
14d). unit quantity library-resource content print
15. schedule of quantities of items used in projects over a period
16. schedule of quantities of materials used in projects over a period

17. schedule of hours of manpower used in projects over a period
18. schedule of hours of plant used in projects over a period
19. schedule of quantities of p.c. components used in projects over a period
20. schedule of items used in unit quantities (i.e. in which units each item appears)

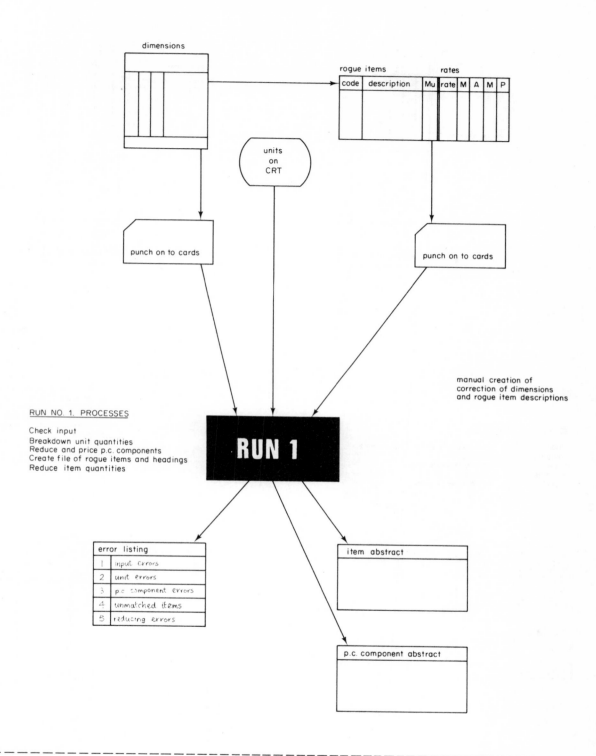

dimensions

rogue items   rates

code	description	Mu	rate	M	A	M	P

units
on
CRT

punch on to cards

punch on to cards

manual creation of
correction of dimensions
and rogue item descriptions

RUN NO. 1. PROCESSES

Check input
Breakdown unit quantities
Reduce and price p.c. components
Create file of rogue items and headings
Reduce item quantities

RUN 1

error listing

1	input errors
2	unit errors
3	p.c. component errors
4	unmatched items
5	reducing errors

item abstract

p.c. component abstract

OPTIONAL PRINT OUTS

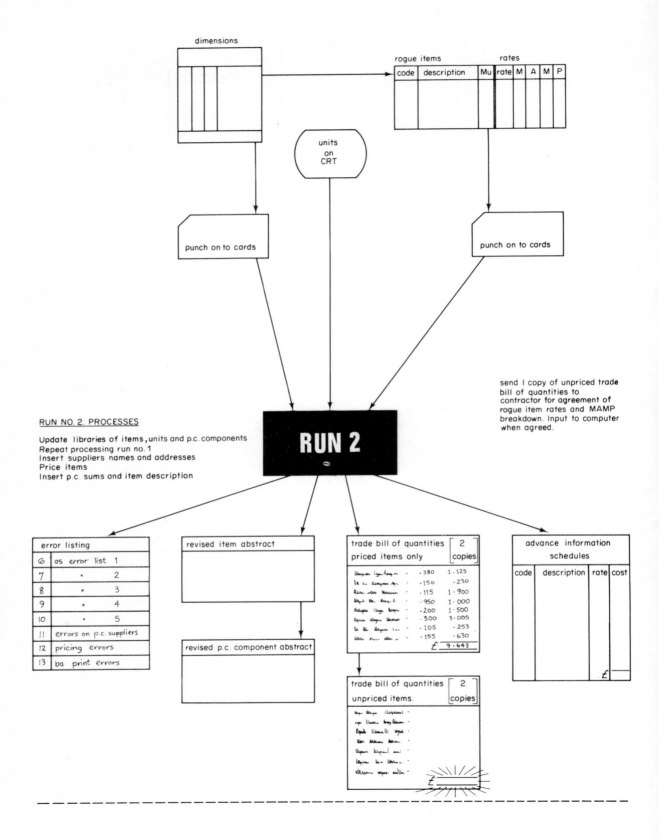

dimensions

rogue items | **rates**

code	description	Mu	rate	M	A	M	P

units
on
CRT

punch on to cards

punch on to cards

send I copy of unpriced trade bill of quantities to contractor for agreement of rogue item rates and MAMP breakdown. Input to computer when agreed.

RUN NO. 2. PROCESSES

Update libraries of items, units and p.c. components
Repeat processing run no. 1
Insert suppliers names and addresses
Price items
Insert p.c. sums and item description

RUN 2

error listing

6	as error list 1
7	" 2
8	" 3
9	" 4
10	" 5
11	errors on p.c. suppliers
12	pricing errors
13	ba print errors

revised item abstract

revised p.c. component abstract

trade bill of quantities ⌐2 copies⌐
priced items only

		.380	1·125
		·150	·230
		·115	1·900
		·950	1·000
		·200	1·500
		·300	3·005
		·105	·253
		·155	·630
		£	9·643

trade bill of quantities ⌐2 copies⌐
unpriced items.

£ _____

advance information schedules

code	description	rate	cost
			£

186

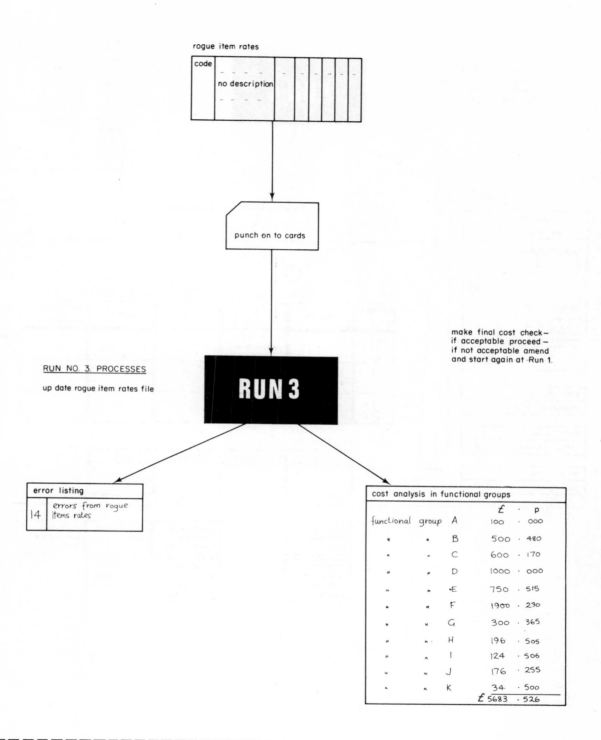

rogue item rates

code	... ...			...	...	...	...	...	
	no description								
	... ...								

punch on to cards

make final cost check —
if acceptable proceed —
if not acceptable amend
and start again at Run 1.

RUN NO. 3. PROCESSES

up date rogue item rates file

RUN 3

error listing

14	errors from rogue items rates

cost analysis in functional groups

			£	·	p
functional	group	A	100	·	000
"	"	B	500	·	480
"	"	C	600	·	170
"	"	D	1000	·	000
"	"	·E	750	·	515
"	"	F	1900	·	230
"	"	G	300	·	365
"	"	H	196	·	505
"	"	I	124	·	506
"	"	J	176	·	255
"	"	K	34	·	500
		£	5683	·	526

full bill of quantities in functional groups

187

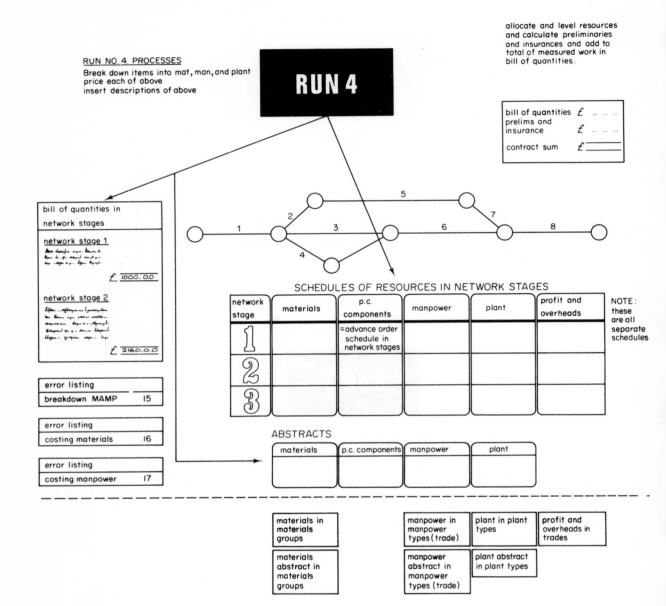

RUN NO. 4. PROCESSES
Break down items into mat, man, and plant
price each of above
insert descriptions of above

RUN 4

allocate and level resources
and calculate preliminaries
and insurances and add to
total of measured work in
bill of quantities.

bill of quantities	£	.. ..
prelims and insurance	£	.. ..
contract sum	£	————

bill of quantities in
network stages

network stage 1

£ 1000.00

network stage 2

£ 2160.0.0

5

2

1   3

4   6   7   8

| error listing | |
| breakdown MAMP | 15 |

| error listing | |
| costing materials | 16 |

| error listing | |
| costing manpower | 17 |

SCHEDULES OF RESOURCES IN NETWORK STAGES

network stage	materials	p.c. components	manpower	plant	profit and overheads
1		=advance order schedule in network stages			
2					
3					

NOTE: these are all separate schedules

ABSTRACTS

materials	p.c. components	manpower	plant

| materials in materials groups |
| materials abstract in materials groups |

| manpower in manpower types (trade) | plant in plant types | profit and overheads in trades |
| manpower abstract in manpower types (trade) | plant abstract in plant types | |

188

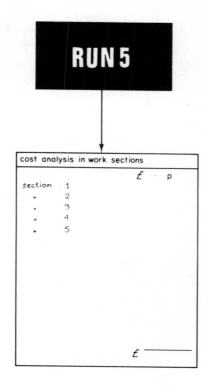

RUN 5

cost analysis in work sections

£ · p

section 1
" 2
" 3
" 4
" 5

£ ───────

- -

full bill of quantities in work sections

REFERENCES

ARCHITECTS' JOURNAL (1968) *Computer Development in West Sussex.*
February 21 and February 28 issue. (1968) *A. J. Information library,*
7 August, 14 August, 21 August and 28 August (1971). Information
Sheet Enclosure I, 4 August, Architectural Press, LONDON.

BROADBENT, G. (1973) *Design in Architecture.* Wiley, LONDON.

BUILDING SPECIFICATION (1971) *Eastergate Primary School, near
Chichester, Sussex.* pp. 34, 35, 36. June 1971 issue. Industrial Publications Ltd., DUBLIN

CHOMSKY, N. (1976) *Reflections on Language.* Temple Smith, LONDON.

COOLEY, M. J. E. (1972) *Computer Aided Design – Its Nature and Implications.* AUEW (TASS) RICHMOND, Surrey.

CONSEIL INTERNATIONAL du BÂTIMENT (1964) *A Master List of Properties for Building Materials and Products.* (1972) *C.I.B. Master Lists
for Structuring Documents Relating to Buildings, Building Elements,
Components, Materials and Products.* International Council for Building Research Studies and Documentation, ROTTERDAM.

FEYERABEND, P. (1975) *Against Method,* NLB, LONDON.

FINE, B. (1974) *Economics of Construction – Tendering Strategy.*
Building pps. 115 – 121 October 1974, LONDON

GORDON A. (1966) *Progression of Architects' Office Libraries.* CARDIFF.

GOSLING, N. 'Absurd Apostle' article 14 May 1972 *The Observer,* Observer
Ltd., LONDON.

GREGORY, R. (1974) *Concepts and Mechanisms of Perception.* Duck-
worth, LONDON. (1967) *Eye and Brain: The Psychology of Seeing.*
Weidenfeld and Nicolson, LONDON.

HER MAJESTY'S STATIONERY OFFICE (1975) *Develop and Construct.*
Compiled by Hutton and Rostron. Published by H.M.S.O. for the
Property Services Agency of the Department of the Environment. Describes a contract procedure developed by the group in P.S.A. responsible
for married quarters design for the armed services. H.M.S.O, LONDON.

HUTTON, G. and ROSTRON, M. (1974) *Computer Programs for the
Building Industry,* 1974, Architectural Press/McGraw Hill, LONDON.

I.B.M. U.K. Ltd. (1971) *The Building System,* I.B.M. U.K., LONDON.

JONES, J. C. (1970) *Design Methods,* Wiley, LONDON.

KAHN, H. and WIENER, J. (1967) *The Year 2000,* MacMillan Publishing
Co., Inc., NEW YORK.

KOESTLER, A. (1964) *The Act of Creation,* Hutchinson, LONDON.

KURENT, T. (1971) *The Roman Modular Way,* pp. 911 *et seq,* December.
Official Architecture and Planning, LONDON.

LEE, R. (1976) *Building Maintenance Management*, Crosby Lockwood Staples, LONDON.

MORRIS, D. (1967) *The Naked Ape*, Johnathan Cape, LONDON.

PUBLIC WORKS CONGRESS (1974) MOSS. A *Modelling System for Highway Design and Related Disciplines*, Craine, Houlton and Malcolmson, The Public Works and Municipal Services Congress Council, LONDON.

ROYAL INSTITUTE OF BRITISH ARCHITECTS (1968) *Towards Computer-aided Building Design*, R.I.B.A. Publications, LONDON. (1976) *Glossary*, R.I.B.A. Journal, January 1976. R.I.B.A. Publications, LONDON.

SCOTTISH FARM BUILDINGS INVESTIGATION UNIT (1969) Farm Building Report, The Environmental Complex in Livestock Housing, Scottish Farm Buildings Investigation Unit, ABERDEEN.

SLOUGH ESTATES LTD. (1976) *Industrial Investment, A Case Study in Factory Building*. Slough Estates Ltd. SLOUGH.

TAVISTOCK INSTITUTE (1965) *Communications in the Building Industry: A study of the Building Industry*. (1966) *Interdependence and Uncertainty: A Study of the Building Industry*. Tavistock Publications, LONDON.

TOFFLER, *1970 Future Shock*. Bodley Head Ltd.

WEST SUSSEX COUNTY COUNCIL, *Program Documentation and Communications Module*. W.S.C.C. CHICHESTER.

ACKNOWLEDGEMENTS TO AUTHORS AND PUBLISHERS

I wish to acknowledge co-operation by the following, in granting permission for diagrams, tables and passages of text to be used from their various publications:

Architects' Journal.
  Quotations from Information Sheet Enclosure 1.
  Dimensional Co-ordination, pp 265 – 266, issue 4/8/71
  Technical Study Enclosure 1, issue 21/7/71
  Illustration on p. 270, issue 4/8/71

Built Environment Quarterly, previously known as *O.A.P.*
  Quotations from pp 911, 912 and 913, *O.A.P.*, December 1971 Building (Publishers) Ltd.
  Quotations from pp. 115 – 121, 25/10/74 *Economics of Construction – Tendering Strategy* by Fine, B.
Cooley, M. J. E. Past President A.U.E.W. – TASS.
  Quotations from p.89 Computer Aided Design, its nature and implications. Published by A.U.E.W. (Technical and Supervisory Section).

Alex Gordon, Quotation from *Progression of Architects' Office Libraries.*

Her Majesty's Stationery Office.
  Reuse of illustrations on Page 3 of *Develop and Construct* published by H.M.S.O. for the Property Services Agency of the Department of the Environment, describing a contract procedure developed by the group in P.S.A. responsible for married quarters design for the armed services.

International Business Machines United Kingdom Ltd., reproduction of the Building System. *System Features,* April 1971.

Tine Kurent.
  Quotations and Illustrations from pp. 911, 912 and 913 of article entitled 'The Roman Modular Way', published in *O.A.P.*, December 1971.

MacMillan Publishing Co. Inc.
  Quotation from page 1 of *The Year 2000* by Kahn, H. and Wiener, J.

N.L.B. Ltd.
 Quotations from pp. 30 and 35, *Against Method*, by Feyerabend, P.

The Observer.
 Quotations from 'Absurd Apostle', by Gosling, N. Public Works and
 Municipal Services Congress Council, and the MOSS consortium
 (Northumberland C.C., Durham C.C., West Sussex C.C.) *Booklet No. 7.*

Royal Institute of British Architects Journal.
 Quotations from *Towards Computer Aided Building Design* and from
 January 1974 issue of Journal.

Scottish Farm Buildings Investigation Unit.
 Quotation and illustration (Figure 6) from Farm's Building Report:
 The Environmental Complex in Livestock Housing. Nov. 1969.

West Sussex County Council.
 Quotations and Illustrations from documents including *Program
 Documentation and Contract Module.*

John Wiley and Son Ltd.
 Quotations from pps. 35 and 36, 41, 42 *Design Methods* by Jones, C.
 pp. *260, 335, 393, 395, Design in Architecture,* Broadbent, G.

NAME INDEX

SUBJECT INDEX

CLIENT/USER

POLICY

INFORMATION
(including computer processing)

EXAMINE

A) IF BUILDING REQUIRED
B) IF NEW BUILDING REQUIRED
C) RESOURCES REQUIRED AND AVAILABLE
D) TIMESCALE
E) POLICY FOR PROJECT

CLIENT/USER INPUT

AGREEMENT OBTAINED

INPUT DECISIONS ON ABOVE

EXAMINE OFFICE RESOURCE NETWORK AND PRODUCE PRELIMINARY PROGRAMME AND ENTER INTO DIARY PROGRAM — 1

ALLOCATE PROJECT TO DESIGN TEAM — 2

DESIGN

INTERACTION WITH CLIENT USER TO DEVELOP BRIEF AND PROGRAMME

OBTAIN SITE DETAILS — 3
COLLECT RELEVANT REGULATIONS, CODES, ETC. — 4
PREPARE FOR DESIGN NEEDS
PROCESS SITE DETAILS — 5
ACTIVATE LOCATION / METEOROLOGICAL SEARCH AND COMPATIBILITY PROGRAM — 6

DATA ON ACTIVITIES, LOCATION AND SITE OBTAINED FROM INFORMATION

INPUT NUMBER OF PEOPLE AND THEIR ACTIVITIES

PROCESS AND PRODUCE SORTATIONS — 7

COMPUTER SORTATIONS EXAMINED AND VARIOUS PERMUTATIONS EXPLORED IN TRADITIONAL MANNER AGAIN BACKGROUND OF FUNCTIONAL REQUIREMENTS OF LOCATION

INPUT DESIRED SORTATION

PRODUCE BUBBLE DIAGRAM

DESIGN TEAM CONSIDER BUBBLE DIAGRAM AND DISCUSS WITH CLIENT
AGREE BUDGET
FUNCTIONAL STANDARD
NEED FOR ESTABLISHING CONTRACTOR & CRITERIA

INFORMATION SENDS OUT MpAMPI DETAILS TO CONTRACTORS AND OBTAINS PERCENTAGE AND INFORMS DESIGN — 8

DESIGN OBTAINS DETAILS OF CONTRACTORS TENDERS & GETS CLIENTS AGREEMENT OF CONTRACTOR — 9

DESIGN PREPARES PROVISIONAL LAYOUT

ACTIVATE COMPUTER TO ANALYSE FUNCTIONAL CRITERIA AS OUTCOME OF PLACING GIVEN ACTIVITIES IN RELATION TO EACH OTHER AND TO THEIR LOCATION — 10

DESIGN TEAM CONSIDERS DATA SUPPLIED FROM INFORMATION AND MAKES HYPOTHESIS. AT THIS STAGE, DESIGN TEAM, CLIENT/USER & COMPUTER WORK TOGETHER INTERACTIVELY. IDEAS ARE INPUT TO MACHINE BASED ON DATA SUPPLIED & THE COMPUTER GIVES IMMEDIATE EVALUATION OF PROPOSED BUILDING SHAPES IN TERMS OF COST, COST IN USE ITEMS SUCH AS ENERGY CONSUMPTION, MAINTENANCE ETC AND ALSO PERFORMANCE SUCH AS ENVIRONMENTAL PERFORMANCE.

INTERACTIVE COMPUTING — 11

CLIENT/USER & DESIGN TEAM AGREE PRELIMINARY DESIGN FOR FINAL EVALUATION

COMPUTER PROCESSES DESIGN DECISIONS & SUPPLIES TO DESIGN, COST BASED ON TENDER — 12